Revising
Business
Prose

SCRIBNER ENGLISH SERIES

Revising Business Prose

Richard A. Lanham

University of California, Los Angeles

Charles Scribner's Sons

New York

Some material in this book appeared in slightly different form in
Revising Prose by Richard Lanham, copyright © 1979 Richard A.
Lanham.

Library of Congress Cataloging in Publication Data

Lanham, Richard A
    Revising business prose.

    1. English language—Style. I. Title.
PE1421.L2965   808′.066651′021   80-26689
ISBN 0-684-17018-3
ISBN 0-684-16861-8 pbk

3 5 7 9 11 13 15 17 19   F/P   20 18 16 14 12 10 8 6 4 2

1 3 5 7 9 11 13 15 17 19 F/HC 20 18 16 14 12 10 8 6 4 2

Printed in the United States of America

CONTENTS

PREFACE

We are all bureaucrats these days, or shortly will be, whether we work for government directly or work in the private sector and get our government money through grants, contracts, or subsidies. And even if we belong to that shrinking part of the private sector that remains really private, we'll be for certain filling out government forms, doing business in a bureaucratic universe. This bureaucratization of the world has created a new language, one that we might call "The Official Style." It has a dozen other "ese" names — Federalese, Bureaucratese, Sociologese, Educationese — depending on what department of the Great Conglomerate we happen to find ourselves in, but it is basically the same language wherever it occurs. Built on the same central imbalance, the atrophy of verbs and the dominance of nouns, it testifies everywhere to the same bureaucratic triumph of stasis over action.

All of us have to act on the basis of it, nevertheless, and to do so we have to translate it into plain speech. If "initiation of the termination process is now considered appropriate" *re* us, we have to know that we're going to be looking for another job. And some of us may also practice this kind of translation in the name of business efficiency, verbal aesthetics, or plain cultural sanity. But whatever our attitude toward The Official Style, we all must do business with — and sometimes in — it.

People think this "plague" of bureaucratic writing is hard to cure. Not so. Nothing is easier — if you want to cure it. The Paramedic Method suggested here provides just the emergency therapy needed — a quick, self-teaching method of revision for people who want to translate bureaucratic prose, their own or someone else's, into plain English. But it is just that — a first aid kit. It's not the art of medicine. Like paramedicine in under-developed countries, it does not attempt to teach a full body of knowledge but only to diagnose and cure the epidemic disease. It won't answer the big question: having the cure, how do you know when, or if, you should take it? For this you need the art of medicine, and for prose style this means a mature training in verbal self-awareness, coupled with wide reading and continued writing. *Revising Business Prose* offers something considerably less ambitious, not a liberal education or even a Bureaucratic Muse, but only a specific method for a specific problem.

We'll begin with some nuts-and-bolts details of sentence shape, rhythm, and emphasis, and then try to focus The Official Style as a whole, ask what it is and does and why it came about. Finally we'll consider briefly the central question — when to use The Official Style and when to leave it alone. I'm trying to make you hyper-conscious about The Official Style. After all, you can't hit what you can't see. Since people no longer seem to know much grammar, I've included the basic terms in an Appendix. All the prose examples, by the way — the "Jim kicks Bill" paradigm excepted — come from real writing in what, with some exaggeration, we call "the real world."

A word on the Paramedic Method — PM. It works only if you *follow* it rather than *argue* with it. When it tells you to get rid of the prepositional phrases, get rid of them. Don't go into a "but, well, in this case, given my style, really I need to . . ." bob and weave. You'll never learn anything that way. The PM constitutes the center of this book. Use it. It's printed in full on the next page; clip it out and tack it above your desk for easy reference.

ACKNOWLEDGMENTS

The original *Revising Prose* (1978) was addressed to a general student audience. It has come to be widely used, however, as a revision manual by people working in business and government, or students who plan to. Several of these readers have asked for a version of the book addressed directly to them and as short as possible. So this adaptation. The examples in this version come from some of the business and government contexts in which the book has been used. The arrangement differs from the original version; the Paramedic Method remains the same.

I must thank Dr. Carol Hartzog of the UCLA Writing Programs and Professor David Mellinkoff of the UCLA School of Law for suggestions about the adaptation.

R. A. L.

Revising Business Prose

1. Circle the prepositions.
2. Circle the "is" forms.
3. Ask "Who is kicking Who?"
4. Put this "kicking" action in a simple (not compound) active verb.
5. Start fast — no mindless introductions.
6. Write out each sentence on a blank sheet of paper and mark off its basic rhythmic units with a "/".
7. Read the passage aloud with emphasis and feeling.
8. Mark off sentence lengths in the passage with a "/".

CHAPTER ONE

Who's Kicking Who?

No responsible official these days would feel comfortable writing simply "Jim kicks Bill." The system seems to require something like "One can easily see that a kicking situation is being implemented between Bill and Jim." Or, "This is the kind of situation in which Jim is a kicker and Bill is a kickee." Jim cannot enjoy kicking Bill; no, for official use, it must be "Kicking Bill is an ongoing activity hugely enjoyed by Jim." Absurdly contrived examples? Here are some real ones:

This office is in need of a dynamic manager of sales.

After reviewing the research and in light of the relevant information found within the context of the conclusions, we feel that there is definite need for some additional research to more specifically pinpoint our advertising and marketing strategies.

Normal belief is that the preparation and submission of a proposal in response to a Request for Proposal (RFP), Request for Quotation (RFQ), or a bid in response to an Invitation for Bids (IFB) is no different than that of an unsolicited proposal for a grant from the National Science Foundation or another government agency; and that if such a proposal or bid is hand-delivered to the Office of Extramural Support on a Friday afternoon, it will get mailed the same day to reach Washington, D.C. by 4:00 p.m. of the following Monday. Having read this article, however, the reader, we hope, will agree that this is an erroneous belief which has led and, if continued to be believed, will lead to unhappy experiences for all concerned.

See what they have in common? They are like our Bill and Jim examples, assembled from strings of prepositional phrases glued together by that all-purpose epoxy "is." In each case the sentence's verbal force has been shunted into a noun and for a verb we make do with "is," the neutral copulative, the weakest verb in the language. Such sentences project no life, no vigor. They just "are." And the "is" generates those strings of prepositional phrases fore and aft. It's so easy to fix. Look for the real action. Ask yourself, who's kicking who? (Yes, I know, it should be *whom,* but doesn't it sound stilted?)

In "This office is in need of a dynamic manager of sales," the action obviously lies in "need." And so, "This office needs a dynamic sales manager." The needless prepositional phrase, "in need of," simply disappears once we see who's kicking who. The sentence, animated by a real verb, comes alive, and in seven words instead of eleven. (If you've not paid attention to your own writing before, think of a lard factor (LF) of 1/3 to 1/2 as normal and don't stop revising until you've removed it.) The lard factor is found by dividing the difference between the number of words in the original and the revision by the number of words in the original—in this case:

$$11 - 7 = 4 \div 11 = 0.36 \text{ or } 36\%$$

We now have the beginnings of the Paramedic Method:

1. Circle the prepositions.
2. Circle the "is" forms.

3. Ask "Who is kicking Who?"
4. Put this "kicking" action in a simple (not compound) active verb.

What about the second example?

After reviewing the research and (in) light (of) the relevant information found (within) the context (of) the conclusions, we feel that there (is) definite need (for) some additional research to more specifically pinpoint our advertising and marketing strategies.

The standard formula: "is" + prepositional phrases fore and aft. Who's kicking Who here? Well, the kicker is obviously "we." And the action? "Needing," just as in the previous example, and here buried down in "there is a definite need for." So the core of the sentence emerges as "We need more research." Let's revise what comes before and after this central statement.

After reviewing the research *of previous* and in light of the relevant information found within the context of the conclusions we feel that there is a definite *suggest that* need for some additional *more* research to more specifically pinpoint our advertising and marketing strategies.

The completed revision then reads:

The conclusions of previous research suggest that we

need more research to pinpoint our advertising and marketing strategies.

18 words instead of 38—LF 53%. Not bad—but wait a minute. How about "the conclusions of"? Do we really need it? Why not just:

> Previous research suggests that we need more research to pinpoint our advertising and marketing strategies. (LF 60%)

And this revision, as so often happens, suggests a further and more daring one:

> has failed
> Previous research ~~suggests that we need more research~~
>
> to pinpoint our advertising and marketing strategies.
>
> (LF 71%)

By now, of course, we've changed kicker and kickee and, to an extent, the meaning. But isn't the new meaning what the writer really wanted to say in the first place? A previous failure has generated a subsequent need? And the new version *sounds* better, too. The awkward repetition of "research" has been avoided and we've finally found the real first kicker, "Previous research," and found out what it was doing—"failed." We can now bring in the second kicker in an emphatic second sentence:

> Previous research has failed to pinpoint our advertising and marketing strategies. *We need to know more.*

No "is," no prepositional phrases, a LF of 58%, and the two actors and actions clearly sorted out.

The drill for this problem stands clear. Circle every form of "to be" (e.g., "is," "was," "will be," "seems to be") and every prepositional phrase. Then find out Who's kicking Who and start rebuilding the sentence with that action. Two prepositional phrases in a row turn on the warning light, three make a problem, and four invite disaster.

With a little practice, sentences like

"The role of markets is easily observed and understood when dealing with a simple commodity such as potatoes."

will turn into

"Examining a simple commodity like potatoes shows clearly how markets work." (LF 39%)

And you will just not commit our third example, the Normative Official Sentence, the pure formula. Maybe a diagram will help:

Normal belief *is* that the preparation and submission
   of a proposal
   in response
   to a Request
   for Proposal (RFP), Request
   for Quotation (RFQ),
   or a bid
   in response
   to an Invitation
   for Bids (IFB)
is no different than that
   of an unsolicited proposal
   for a grant
   from the National Science Foundation

and if such a proposal or bid *is* hand-delivered
> *to* the Office
> *of* Extramural Support
> *on* a Friday afternoon

it will get mailed the same day to reach Washington, D.C.
> *by* 4:00 p.m.
> *of* the following Monday.

Strings of prepositional phrases, glued together by "is's." Since each prepositional phrase depends on the one preceding, we soon lose track of Who's kicking Who. But down there in the murk glimmers the verb "differ."

> "Unsolicited grant proposals differ from ones solicited by a Request for Proposal (RFP), a Request for Quotation (RFQ), or an Invitation for Bids (IFB)."

For the rest of the passage we need a second sentence. Here the action lies buried in "Normal belief is that" and in "will lead to unhappy experiences for all concerned." You want to make these actions clear. How about this?

> If you bring a solicited proposal to our office on Friday afternoon, thinking it will be mailed that day and reach Washington by Monday at 4:00 p.m., you'll be disappointed. We hope this article has shown you why.

The revision aims at spotlighting the action, making clear *what's happening* and *to whom*. Once you've done this, once you see the bones of the sentence, the fat is easier to remove. Again, here is the entire original, and then the revision.

ORIGINAL

Normal belief is that the preparation and submission of a proposal in response to a Request for Proposal (RFP), Request for Quotation (RFQ), or a bid in response to an Invitation for Bids (IFB) is no different than that of an unsolicited proposal for a grant from the National Science Foundation or another government agency; and that if such a proposal or bid is hand-delivered to the Office of Extramural Support on a Friday afternoon, it will get mailed the same day to reach Washington, D.C. by 4:00 p.m. of the following Monday. Having read this article, however, the reader, we hope, will agree that this is an erroneous belief which has led and, if continued to be believed, will lead to unhappy experiences for all concerned.

REVISION

Unsolicited grant proposals differ from ones solicited by a Request for Proposal (RFP), a Request for Quotation (RFQ), or an Invitation for Bids (IFB). If you bring a solicited proposal to our offices on Friday afternoon, thinking it will be mailed that day and reach Washington by Monday at 4:00 p.m., you'll be disappointed. We hope this article has shown you why. (LF 54%).

The Normative Official Sentence does not, to be fair, always come from bureaucrats. Look at these "of" strings from a communications theorist, a literary critic, and a popular gourmet:

It is the totality *of* the interrelation *of* the various components *of* language and the other communication systems which is the basis for referential memory.

These examples *of* unusual appropriateness *of* the sense *of* adequacy to the situation suggest the primary signification *of* rhyme in the usual run *of* lyric poetry.

Frozen breads and frozen pastry completed the process *of* depriving the American woman *of* the pleasure *of* boasting *of* her baking.

These "of" strings are the worst. They remind you of a child pulling a gob of bubble gum out into a long string. When you try to revise them, you can feel how fatally easy the "is and of" formulation can be for expository prose. And how fatally confusing, too, since to find an active, transitive verb for "is" means, often, adding a specificity the writer has not provided. So, in the first example, what does "is the basis for" really mean? And does the writer mean that language's components interact with "other communication systems," or is he talking about "components" of "other communication systems" as well? The "of" phrases refer back to those going before in so general a way that you can't keep straight what really modifies what. So revision here, alas, is partly a guess.

ORIGINAL

It is the totality of the interrelation of the various components of language and the other communication systems which is the basis for referential meaning.

REVISION #1

Referential meaning emerges when the components of language interact with other communication systems.

Or the sentence might mean:

REVISION #2

Referential meaning emerges when the components of language interact with the components of other communications systems.

Do you see the writer's problem? He has tried to be more specific than he needs to be, to build his sentence on a noun ("totality") which demands a string of "of's" to qualify it. Ask where the action is, build the sentence on a *verb*, and the "totality" follows as an implication.

The second example shows even more clearly how an "of" string can blur what goes with what. Do the first two prepositional phrases ("of the sense of adequacy") form a unit which refers back to "appropriateness"? That is, something like this:

These examples of unusual appropriateness *of the sense of adequacy,* to the

situation suggest . . .

Or are we to take all three prepositional phrases as a sub-unit which refers back to "appropriateness"? Something like this:

These examples of unusual appropriateness *of the sense of adequacy to the situation,* suggest . . .

No way to tell, and the irresolution between the two blurs our vision. Taking such a sentence out of context doesn't help, of course, but even in context we'd stop and blink to clear our eyes. Here's the original again and my best guess for a revision:

ORIGINAL

These examples of unusual appropriateness of the sense of adequacy to the situation suggest the primary signification of rhyme in the usual run of lyrical poetry.

REVISION

These examples, where adequacy to the situation seems unusually appropriate, suggest how rhyme usually works in lyric poetry.

The third passage is much easier to fix:

ORIGINAL

Frozen breads and frozen pastry completed the process of depriving the American woman of the pleasure of boasting of her baking.

REVISION

No longer, after frozen breads and pastry, could the American woman boast about her baking.

In asking Who's kicking Who, a couple of mechanical tricks come in handy. Besides getting rid of the "is's" and changing every passive voice ("is defended by") to an active voice ("defends"), you can squeeze the compound verbs hard, make every "are able to" turn into a "can," every "seems to succeed in creating" into "creates," every "cognize the fact that" (no, I didn't make it up) into "think," every "am hopeful that" into "hope," every "provides us with an example of" into "exemplifies," every "seeks to reveal" into "shows," every "there is the inclusion of" into "includes."

And you can amputate those mindless introductory phrases, "The fact of the matter is that" and "The nature of the case is that." Start fast and then, as they say in the movies, "Cut to the chase." Instead of "The answer is in the negative," you'll find yourself saying "No."

We now can add a rule to the Paramedic Method (PM):

1. Circle the prepositions.
2. Circle the "is" forms.
3. Ask "Who is kicking Who?"
4. Put this "kicking" action in a simple (not compound) active verb.
5. Start fast—no mindless introductions.

Let's try out this PM on some samples of the Official Style. We want plain language nonfat versions half as long and with some zip.

The Official Style is often used to cover up things you'd rather not say at all. One of Ted Kennedy's aides, for example, was asked if the race against Jimmy Carter for the 1980 Democratic nomination was proving harder than expected. He couldn't give a straight "yes" or "no" answer—*nobody* in Washington does that—and so translated the question into the Official Style:

> The intellectual appreciation (of) the difficulty (was) not
>
> (up to) the reality.

I've done steps 1 and 2 of the PM. For #3—Who's kicking Who—we have to add a kicker, a *person* performing an *act,* since none is provided: "The intellectual appreciation was not up to" = "We didn't *understand.*" For the kickee, add "how hard it would actually be" = "We didn't understand how hard it would actually be." We've complied with rule #4—simple verb form—and rule #5, too—Start fast. Notice how slow off the mark the original is? Six words before you get to a verb and then only a lifeless "was."

Now, in a slightly longer passage, we move to advertising. Read it over and sketch out for yourself how the revision should proceed. Then we'll work through it sentence by sentence.

> The first project that should be undertaken should obtain a measure of the acceptability of the product's *taste* and *usage*. If the majority of the consumers express dissatisfaction with the product's taste, then attempts to establish the current product are doomed. Product taste and usage are especially critical for the sweetener. If there is significant negative reaction to the taste, then changes in the recipe would be recommended. If there was confusion about the suitability of granulated flavoring for use as a topping or spread, then one of the major goals of advertising would be to educate the public on the product's use. Research on consumer reaction to the product is essential to answer several of the basic questions about how to best market this new product.

We can fix the first sentence by simple subtraction:

> The first project ~~that should be undertaken~~ should ~~obtain a~~ measure ~~of~~ the acceptability of the product's taste and usage.

Kicker: "first project"; action: "measure"; kickee: "acceptability". (LF 30%) The revision now reads:

> The first project should measure the acceptability of the product's *taste* and *usage*.

The second sentence requires more work:

> If the majority of the consumers express dissatisfaction with the product's taste, then attempts to establish the current product are doomed.

Not an egregious example of The Official Style, this, but dead, lifeless. It couldn't inspire anyone to sell anything. It takes too long to get going and it ends with no emphasis, no zip. The trouble, as always, lies in the verbs—"express dissatisfaction" and "are doomed." How about this revision?

> If consumers don't like the product's taste, it won't sell.

"The majority of" provides a needless specification that slows down the sentence's opening; "Express dissatisfaction with" is a prissy way of saying "don't like"; "then attempts to establish the current product are doomed" is a long-winded way to say "it won't sell." Notice how this windiness drains all the life from the last half of the sentence? And, now that we've gotten this far, the obvious final revision presents itself: "If the product tastes bad, it won't sell."

The rest of the passage offers the basic Official Style pattern—"is" + prepositional phrases—almost entirely. For verb choice, with the exception of one construction—"would be recommended"—only "is" gets the nod. I'll circle the prepositions and underline the "is" forms.

Product taste and usage are especially critical for the

sweetener. If there is significant negative reaction to

the taste, then changes in the recipe would be recommended. If there was confusion about the suitability
of granulated flavoring for use as a topping or spread,
then one of the major goals of advertising would be to
educate the public on the product's use. Research on
consumer reaction to the product is essential to
answer several of the basic questions about how best
to market this new product.

In the revisions which follow, I'm obeying rules 3–5,
asking Who's kicking Who, putting that action in a simple verb, and starting the sentence fast.

ORIGINAL
Product taste and usage are especially critical for the
sweetener.

Here's a classic case of blurring the action. The sentence
seems to say that "Product taste and usage" are doing
something to "the sweetener" when actually, as the passage goes on to explain, it works just the other way
around. The sweetener determines how the product tastes
and is used. Why not just say so?

The sweetener determines how the product tastes and
is used.

The other revisions follow easily, once we have this basic
argument clear:

If ~~there is significant reaction to the~~ <u>people don't like its</u> taste, ~~then changes in the recipe would be recommended.~~ <u>we should change it.</u> If ~~there was confusion about the suitability of~~ <u>they don't know how to use</u> granulated flavoring ~~for use~~ as a topping or spread, then ~~one of the major goals of advertising would be to educate the public on the product's use.~~ <u>our advertising must show them.</u> Research on consumer reaction ~~to the product is essential to~~ <u>must</u> answer ~~several of the~~ <u>these</u> basic questions ~~about how~~ <u>if we are</u> to ~~best~~ market

this new product.

So the whole revision looks like this:

ORIGINAL

The first project that should be undertaken should obtain a measure of the acceptability of the product's *taste* and *usage*. If the majority of the consumers express dissatisfaction with the product's taste, then attempts to establish the current product are doomed. Product taste and usage are especially critical for the sweetener. If there is significant negative reaction to the taste, then changes in the recipe would be recommended. If there was confusion about the suitability of granulated flavoring for use as a topping or spread, then one of the major goals of advertising would be to educate the public on the product's use. Research on consumer reaction to the product is essential to answer several of the basic questions about how to best market this new product.

REVISION

The first project should measure the acceptability of the product's *taste* and *usage*. If consumers don't like the product's taste, it won't sell. The sweetener determines how the product tastes and is used. If people don't like its taste, we should change it. If they don't know how to use granulated flavoring as a topping or spread, then our advertising must show them. Research on consumer reaction must answer these basic questions if we are to market this new product.

Thus de-larded, the passage suggests a further revision: we don't really need the last sentence at all, since it is implied by the first. Just add a "research" before the third word, "project." No need to talk about selling the product as the goal of all this—that's the name of the game.
  So the original and final revision look like this:

ORIGINAL

The first project that should be undertaken should obtain a measure of the acceptability of the product's *taste* and *usage*. If the majority of the consumers express dissatisfaction with the product's taste, then attempts to establish the current product are doomed. Product taste and usage are especially critical for the sweetener. If there is significant negative reaction to the taste, then changes in the recipe would be recommended. If there was confusion about the suitability of granulated flavoring for use as a topping or spread, then one of the major goals of advertising would be to educate the public on the product's use. Research on consumer reaction to the product is essential to answer several of the basic questions about how to best market this new product.

REVISION

The first research project should measure the acceptability of the product's *taste* and *usage*. If the product tastes bad, it won't sell. The sweetener determines how the product tastes and is used. If people don't like its taste, we should change it. If they don't know how to use granulated flavoring as a topping or spread, then advertising must show them. (63 words instead of 127: LF 50%)

Yes, of course this kind of revision is tedious and time-consuming. But, using the PM, you'll soon get good at doing it quickly. Isn't getting on with your business twice as fast worth the effort? And in working, as in the rest of life, it's a big help to know where the action is, Who's really kicking Who. Again, the rules thus far:

1. Circle the prepositions.
2. Circle the "is" forms.
3. Ask "Who is kicking Who?"
4. Put this "kicking" action in a simple (not compound) active verb.
5. Start fast—no mindless introductions.

CHAPTER TWO

Sentences and Shopping Bags

None of the sentences you've just worked through has any shape. They just go on and on, as if they were emerging from a nonstop sausage machine. This shapelessness makes them unreadable: you cannot read them aloud with expressive emphasis. Try to. When language as spoken and heard has completely atrophied, the sentence becomes less a shaped unit of emphatic utterance than a shopping bag of words. Read your own prose aloud and with emphasis—or better still, have a friend read it to you. This rehearsal can often tell you more about failures of shape, rhythm, and emphasis of your sentences than any other single device. You might try, too, writing a single sentence on a sheet of blank paper. Forget meaning for a minute and just look at the sentence's shape. Try to isolate the basic parts and trace their relationship to one another. Looking for the natural shape of a sentence often suggests the quickest way to revision.

When prose is read aloud, the voice can shape and punctuate as it goes along. But when the voice atrophies, the eye does not make the same demands with equal insistence, and the larger shaping rhythms that build through a paragraph tend to blur. A problem hard to see and hard to remedy. Consider this passage from a recent popular article by an American economist:

18

A third advantage of the market as a means of social organization is its "devil-take-the-hindmost" approach to questions of individual equity. At first blush this is an outrageous statement worthy of the coldest heart among the nineteenth-century Benthamites. And obviously I have stated the point in a way more designed to catch the eye than to be precise.

In any except a completely stagnant society, an efficient use of resources requires constant change. Consumer tastes, production technologies, locational advantages, and resource availabilities are always in flux. From the standpoint of static efficiency, the more completely and rapidly the economy shifts production to meet changes in tastes, resource availability or locational advantages, the greater the efficiency. From a dynamic standpoint, the greater the advances in technology and the faster they're adopted, the greater the efficiency. While these changes on balance generate gains for society in the form of higher living standards, almost every one of them causes a loss of income to some firms and individuals, often temporary and for only a few, but sometimes long-lasting and for large numbers.

What do you notice? Well, that first sentence, for a start—an almost perfect Normative Official Sentence, though now from a high government official:

A third advantage
   of the market
   as a means
   of social organization

is its "devil-take-the-hindmost" approach
   to questions
   of individual equity.

Although the sentences do not run to an exact length, they are mostly long and mostly monotonous. No short sentences means no large-scale emphasis, no climax and finality. The last sentence of paragraph one, though much shorter than any other, doesn't summarize anything. How to supply some shape? For a start, get the lard out of the first paragraph:

A (third advantage) ~~of~~ the market as a ~~means of~~ social

organization ~~is~~ *rests in* its "devil-take-the-hindmost" ap-

proach to ~~questions of~~ individual equity. (At first

~~blush~~ this ~~is an~~ outrageous statement, *seems,* worthy of the

coldest (heart.) ~~among the nineteenth century~~ Ben-

thamites. And obviously I have stated the point ~~in a~~

~~way more designed~~ to catch the eye ~~than to be~~

~~precise.~~

What has been done? I've made one assumption the writer did not, that the audience knows "Benthamite" implies "nineteenth-century." Otherwise, only fat has been removed. The rhythm has picked up a little. The first sentence now begins more quickly and it has a real verb (though "rests" may not be ideal—how about "remains" or "stands"?). Phrases like "questions of," "problems of," "factors of" are simply mindless fillers, bad habits like saying "like" and "you know" after every third word. A plain noun, left all by itself, often comes across stronger. The changes in the second sentence all aim to increase the emphasis on "outrageous statement." In the third, I've tried to underscore the parallelism of "stated the point" and "catch the eye."

The original and revision to date:

ORIGINAL

A third advantage of the market as a means of social organization is its "devil-take-the-hindmost" approach to questions of individual equity. At first blush this is an outrageous statement worthy of the coldest heart among the nineteenth-century Benthamites. And obviously I have stated the point in a way more designed to catch the eye than to be precise.

REVISION

The market's third advantage as a social organization rests in its "devil-take-the-hindmost" approach to individual equity. This outrageous statement seems, at first blush, worthy of the coldest Benthamite heart. And obviously I have stated the point to catch the eye. (LF 33%)

Sentence lengths of 19-13-11 instead of 24-18-20. The result may still fall short of greatness, but at least a decreasing-length pattern has begun to form and the last sentence has a bit of zip. Sometimes little changes take you a long way:

In any except a completely stagnant society, an efficient use of resources requires constant change.

Again, the adverbial intensifier ("completely") weakens instead of strengthens. And we want to reach "stagnant society" more quickly. Read the two versions aloud several times. Does the revision succeed in placing more stress on "constant change"? The same desire for end-stress now changes "are always in flux" to "always change" in the next sentence. In the following one:

~~From the standpoint of~~ For static efficiency, the more ~~completely and~~ rapidly the economy shifts production to meet chang~~es~~ing ~~in~~ taste~~s~~, resource~~s~~ ~~availability,~~ or location~~al~~s ~~advantages~~, the ~~greater the efficiency~~ better.

Now we want to preserve the static/dynamic contrast he is developing—"for static efficiency/for dynamic efficiency":

~~From a~~ For dynamic ~~standpoint~~ efficiency, the ~~greater~~ faster the ~~advances~~ ~~in~~ technolog~~y~~ical change ~~and the faster they are adopted~~, the ~~greater the efficiency~~ better.

The two sentences still end with the same phrase, but since they connect more closely the prose no longer sounds like a list or catalogue.

The curse of The Official Style is spelling everything out. The Official Stylist prepares an assertion the way a cook prepares abalone, by beating it repeatedly with a hammer to make it tender. So in the previous sentence, and in the one which follows:

While these changes ~~on balance~~ generate ~~gains for society in the form of~~ higher living standards, almost ~~every one of them causes a loss of~~ *all decrease* income, ~~to some firms and individuals,~~ often temporarily and for ~~only~~ a few, but sometimes ~~long-lasting~~ *permanently* and for ~~large~~ *many* ~~numbers~~. (LF 50%)

The sense may require "on balance," but everything else removed is pure lard. Again, the revision stresses the ending parallelism:

temporarily and for a few
permanently and for many.

Our revision to date, then, reads like this:

The market's third advantage as a social organization rests in its "devil-take-the-hindmost" approach to individual equity. This outrageous statement seems, at first blush, worthy of the coldest Benthamite heart. And obviously I have stated the point to catch the eye.

Except in a stagnant society, efficient use of resources requires constant change. For static efficiency, the more rapidly the economy shifts production to meet changing tastes, resources, or locations, the better. For dynamic efficiency, the faster the technological change, the better. While these changes generate higher living standards, almost all decrease income, often temporarily and for a few, but sometimes permanently and for many. (LF 42%)

A writer who has no feeling for sentence shape encourages himself to be long-winded. Look, for example, at the following bureaucratic genuflection:

A *Directional Transaction* is defined as "an information contact which facilitates the use of the library in which the contact occurs and which does NOT involve the knowledge, use, recommendation, interpretation, or instruction in the use of any information sources other than those which describe *that* library, such as schedules, floor plans, handbooks, and policy statements. Examples of directional transactions include giving directions for locating, within the library, staff, patrons, or physical features; lending pencils, etc.; and giving assistance of a non-bibliographic nature with machines." In the College Library this definition is expanded to include directions for locating the other Units and facilities within the building, such as the Education/Psychology Library, the Newspaper Stacks, the toilets, etc. and the non-library buildings such as Ackerman, Murphy, etc. ALL OTHER QUESTIONS ARE TO BE REFERRED TO THE COLLEGE LIBRARY REFERENCE DESK. Such questions as "Where are the history books?" "Where is the Music Library?" should be answered with, "Please check at the Reference Desk (right at the top of the stairs around the corner, etc.)" or "They have campus maps and floor plans and directories there."

First you notice the ugly sound of all those "shun" words: "directional transaction," "information," "recommendation," "interpretation," "instruction." Then you wonder what the passage means. Imagine showing up for your first day at work in the library and being confronted by this. "Huh?" How to rewrite it so an ordinary person could understand? First, you've got to keep your new employee from getting lost in the strings of "shun" words. For "A Directional Transaction" read "A direction"; for "is defined as" read "means"; for "an information contact which facilitates the use of the library in which the contact occurs" read "answering a question"; a question "which does *not* involve the knowledge, use, recommendation, interpretation, or instruction in the use of any information sources other than those which describe *that* library" seems to mean — if it means anything — "a simple question." What if, applying the PM, we just said, " 'A Direction' means answering a simple question — about schedules, floor plans, rules."? (LF 79%) If the sentence means anything, I suppose it must mean this, but this sounds like — and is — a simple-minded tautology. Our effort to give the sentence a shape has exposed it as tautological nonsense. Concern with shape leads directly to a concern with meaning. Try reading the passage aloud. Wouldn't anybody, even the writer, stop halfway through, lost and bemused? As for the rest of the passage, I don't know. It seems to tell the new employee that, if asked where the Music Library is, s/he mustn't tell *even if s/he knows*. If not, the whole shapeless mess breaks down to "If you can't answer someone's question, refer him/her to a librarian." Shaping a sentence means emphasizing its central assertion. If it asserts nothing, the shaping pressure will soon reveal the vacuum, as here. Shaping is, to borrow a phrase from Hemingway, a great crap detector.

We don't always have to work with such unpromising material, however. Here is a passage from a book on marketing. The prose is not unclear, only lifeless, flat, boring to read. It gives you no help.

As is true of other markets, the most fruitful way of

penetrating the financial markets analytically is to break the subject down into the supply and demand aspects. The problem of doing so in this case is that the same institutions may be supply elements at one time and in one circumstance but demand elements at other times and under differing circumstances. For example, business corporations are important elements in these markets and are usually on the borrowing side of both the money and capital markets. Nevertheless, most large corporations are also important lenders in the money markets.

Here, we need only subtract and rearrange, not gaze into a crystal ball:

As ~~is true of~~ with other markets, ~~the most fruitful way of~~ breaking down ~~penetrating the~~ financial markets ~~analytically is to~~ ~~break the subject down~~ into ~~the~~ supply and demand ~~aspects.~~ makes analysis easier.

The revision puts the central assertion—making analysis easier—at the end of the sentence, where it receives a natural stress. And the revision gets the sentence going faster, too, tightening up the introductory phrase and introducing the important words—"breaking" and "financial markets"—sooner. Do you notice how meaningless fillers like "aspects" blur the words they are meant to sharpen?

~~The problem of doing so in this case is that~~ But the same institutions may be supply elements at one time and

~~in one~~ circumstance ~~but~~ ^{and} demand elements at ~~other~~ ^{another}

~~times and under differing circumstances~~.

Two things remarkable here. Notice how long the sentence takes to get started? By the time this wind-up is over, we've all stolen second base, and maybe third too. And notice how the words we've excised from the second half of the sentence gave it only a pseudo-precision? They really qualified nothing. Even when the qualifications are genuine, you'll usually do better sacrificing them for a tighter rhythm such as, here, the nice balance of "A at one time; B at another." Often the extra detail offered will, as in this passage, turn out bogus anyway.

(For example,) ~~business~~ corporations, ~~are important~~

~~elements in these markets and are~~ usually ~~on the bor-~~

~~rowing side of~~ both ~~the~~ ^{borrowers in} money and capital markets,

~~Nevertheless, most large corporations~~ are also impor-

tant lenders in the money markets.

Here the original has done just the wrong thing. The two antithetical elements, borrowers and lenders, should be kept close together to give the contrast some zing. Instead, they are sequestered into separate sentences. The revision, by correcting the damage, intensifies the comparison.

> Corporations, for example, usually borrowers in both money and capital markets, are also important lenders in the money markets.

And so the whole passage looks like this:

ORIGINAL

As is true of other markets, the most fruitful way of penetrating the financial markets analytically is to break the subject down into the supply and demand aspects. The problem of doing so in this case is that the same institutions may be supply elements at one time and in one circumstance but demand elements at other times and under differing circumstances. For example, business corporations are important elements in these markets and usually on the borrowing side of both the money and capital markets. Nevertheless, most large corporations are also important lenders in the money markets.

REVISION

As with other markets, breaking down financial markets into supply and demand makes analysis easier. But the same institutions may be supply elements at one time and circumstance and demand elements at another. Corporations, for example, usually borrowers in both money and capital markets, are also important lenders in the money markets. (LF 47%)

Much of the awkwardness we've been chronicling comes from an exaggerated desire for precision. The authors spell everything out. If we number every streak of the tulip, somehow that will make instantly clear what the tulip is like, focus essence through an enumeration of particulars. So in the following piece of workaday prose:

MOTOR VEHICLE SAFETY STANDARD NO. 217
Bus Window Retention and Release
(Docket No. 2-10; Notice 3)

The standard requires emergency exit location markings to be placed in certain occupant spaces because of a possible contradiction under the proposed standard between the requirement that the identification markings be located within 6 inches of the point of operation and the requirement that the markings be visible to a seated occupant. The NHTSA has concluded that emergency egress could be hindered if the passenger has difficulty in finding the marking, and that location of the marking outside of an occupant space containing an adjacent seat, which could be permitted under the proposed standard, could create this problem. At the same time it is desirable for the identification and instructions to be located near the point of release. Therefore the final rule requires that when a release mechanism is not located within an occupant space containing an adjacent seat, a label indicating the location of the nearest release mechanism shall be placed within the occupant space.

Lots of problems here — the "is + prep. phrase" habit, the shopping-bag shape, and especially a wonderful bureaucratic fondness for spelling out the obvious, as in "emergency egress could be hindered if the passenger has difficulty in finding the marking."

But above all it lacks *focus*. We don't know which assertions are central, which derivative and subordinate. Again, a problem of Who's kicking Who, but this time on a paragraph as well as a sentence level. Let's try the Paramedic Method here, only this time adding two more diagnostic procedures:

1. Circle the prepositions.
2. Circle the "is" forms.
3. Ask "Who is kicking Who?"
4. Put this "kicking" action in a simple (not compound) active verb.
5. Start fast — no mindless introductions.
6. Write out each sentence on a blank sheet of paper and mark off its basic rhythmic units with a "/".
7. Read the passage aloud with emphasis and feeling.

I'm not sure, though, what the passage means. No cheap shot intended; writing this kind of detailed instruction is hard. If I've mistaken the meaning in my revision, try one of your own.

Here goes. We are in a bus, trying to decide where to put the emergency exit signs that indicate a pop-out window. Standard No. 217 requires that in addition to the emergency exit signs placed next to the pop-out windows themselves, signs pointing to the exits be placed in rows of seats not next to pop-out windows. Thus everyone not sitting next to an exit window will be directed to one. A good deal of specific detail accompanies this central rule. What we need, then, is a short and emphatic opening sentence which will tell us what we're doing. Notice how badly the opening sentence does this job. Here it is again:

> The standard requires emergency exit location markings to be placed in certain occupant spaces because of a possible contradiction under the proposed standard between the requirement that the identification markings be located within 6 inches of the point of operation and the requirement that the markings be visible to a seated occupant.

Too many things happening on the same level:

1. Emergency exit location markings have to be placed in

"certain occupant spaces," but those spaces not defined until later—

2. A possible contradiction between the two other requirements—
3. Signs 6″ from window—
4. Signs to be visible to a seated occupant.

Two ways to skin this cat. Either you can start with a causal sequence: The proposed standard requires both (3) and (4) and they conflict. *Therefore* we propose the following. Or you can start with the new standard itself and then explain how it came to be. Let's try both openings and see which is better.

REVISION #1

The proposed standard requires two things: (1) emergency window exit signs must be within 6″ of the window; (2) every seated passenger must be able to see the sign. These two requirements sometimes conflict. If you are sitting in a row of seats not next to an emergency window, you won't be able to see the sign. Standard 217 requires that these rows have a sign directing you to the emergency window.

or,

REVISION #2:

Standard 217 requires that seat rows not next to emergency exit windows include signs directing passengers to the exit windows. The present standard includes two provisions which conflict. First, every emergency window exit must be marked by a sign within 6″ of the window. Second, every seated passenger must be able to see the sign. But what about passengers seated in rows not next to an emergency window? They might not be able to see the sign. NHTSA has concluded that signs should be placed in those rows directing passengers to the emergency windows.

These revisions take care of the first paragraph. Word-counts for the sentences run this way:

Original: 52-46-20-38
Revision #1: 30-5-23-15
Revision #2: 20-8-16-11-13-9-17

The revisions vary the sentence length more but, more important, they make them all shorter. A very long sentence, to stay in your head all at once, has to have a very clear framework. It may use parallelism, parenthesis, contrasts, alliteration, a whole repertoire of patterns. Without these patterns as a guide, the reader soon gets lost. Shorter sentences solve the problem in a different way. In the revisions, the central idea—because two requirements conflict, we need a third—occurs in two different ways but takes a spotlight in both. Which revision is better? The first, probably. Shorter than the second (71 words against 94; LF 54% and 39%), it also uses the short/long focusing strategy better.

The PM revisions have done other things besides vary sentence length, to be sure. The "is" + preposition formula has been broken up, the diction simplified ("location marking" = "sign"), the reader has been re-assigned his humanity ("you" for "occupant"), and the sentences given a little shape. As a result of all these changes, the passage's central assertion seems a little clearer. Maybe we could revise yet again.

REVISION #3

The proposed Standard 217 requires three things: (1) emergency window exit signs must be within 6″ of the window; (2) seated passengers must be able to see the signs; (3) if they can't see the window signs, post an extra sign they can see.

Radical therapy, this. We've left out the "possible contradiction" thread of the argument. But look what has been gained: LF 75%; paragraph reduced to one sentence; above all, *focus*. The regulation's essence leaps to the eye. Sentence shape supplies exactly the kind of specificity needed. Each revision represents a trade-off between emphasis and detail. Wouldn't the third be the best bet if you were writing Standard 217?

Shaping a sentence, then, means focusing an idea. Look at the following shapeless blur:

> We are not anxious to casually spend the company's money but our recommendation is intended to minimize the risk involved in launching a new product and a new category into an environment where there exists a vacuum of current knowledge and interest from both consumer and retailer.

Here the chick struggling out of the egg depends on contrast: a *bad* way to spend the company's money (needless research) versus a *good* way to spend the company's money (research that launches a product with minimum risk). The sentence as written smears this contrast over five lines. Neither eye nor ear gives the mind any help. How do we get these two powerful allies on our side? How about this:

> We don't want to waste the company's money on needless research, but informative research can save money in launching a new product, especially in an unknown market.

We've set up an "X" pattern that brings the contrast to quick visual focus.

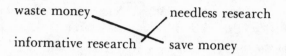

You put contrasted ideas in similar phrases ("waste money" and "save money"; "needless research" and "informative research"). You invert the basic order in the second element—"money . . . research" becomes "research . . . money" to show that you have inverted the cash flow. And the new visual shape invites the voice to point up the contrast, stress "waste" and "needless" in the first element, "informative" and "save" in the second. A little final guff-removal converts "into an environment where there exists a vacuum of current knowledge and interest from both consumer and retailer" into "especially in an unknown market."

Here are original and revision again:

ORIGINAL

We are not anxious to casually spend the company's money but our recommendation is intended to minimize the risk involved in launching a new product and a new category into an environment where there exists a vacuum of current knowledge and interest from both consumer and retailer. (47 words)

REVISION

We don't want to waste the company's money on needless research, but informative research can save money in launching a new product, especially in an unknown market. (27 words)

A sentence whose shape helps launch its idea and a lard factor of 43%—a sentence half as long and twice as good.

And think of the back pressure: writing prose that *sees* clearly may help us to *think* clearly.

Here is another little shopping baglet. But now the blurring comes less from ineptitude than from design:

> As indicated previously, it would be speculative to attempt a prediction of the financial liability of the public airport proprietor in the event it had to bear the financial responsibility for damage under judgments made against it on account of aircraft noise.

Financial liability poses a sticky wicket for this writer of an Environmental Impact Statement. The City Fathers who want to buy the airport hired him to write the report, and they don't want this appalling liability spectre to make the scene. If the writer had been an ordinary citizen and not a hired gun, s/he might have just said, "Nobody has any idea how much money aircraft noise suits could cost the city." But that skillful side-by-side placement of the two parallel central elements—"has any idea" and "how much money"—detonated just the land-mine which the writer has been tiptoeing around. Notice how the eye leads the voice to wrap itself around "has any idea," to raise both pitch and stress when you pronounce it? To avoid this, the writer has taken refuge in the full Official Style. Look again:

> As indicated previously, it would be speculative to attempt a prediction of the financial liability of the public airport proprietor in the event it had to bear the financial responsibility for damage under judgments made against it on account of aircraft noise.

The standard Official Style drill:

1. "To be" verb (here "would be") plus a string of prepositional phrases.
2. Kicker evaporated out of sight in an impersonal construction ("it would be speculative").
3. Real verb *predict* stuffed safely out of sight down in "to attempt a prediction of."
4. Really scary verb (*pay*) really stuffed out of sight in "bear the financial liability for."

The Official Style smears the point out into a 42-word bag. Our common sense version — "Nobody has any idea how much money aircraft-noise suits could cost the city" — focuses the point in 14. (LF 66%)

As a last example of prose shapelessness, look at this attempt by a government official to report on athletic safety:

Sports medicine. — Our investigation of player safety appeared to touch only the surface of a far larger problem which, for short-hand purposes, may be denominated sports medicine. Our inquiries revealed that while there is recognition of the growing problem of injuries and drug abuse in sports, and in this instance the problem is common to amateur as well as professional sports, there appears to be little systematic study of the means and methods to prevent sports injuries or to understand the effects of drugs on athletes and to educate the profession on the proper use of drugs. (98 words)

Sports medicine. — Our investigation of player safety
exposed
~~appeared to touch only the surface of~~ a ~~far~~ larger prob-

lem~~, which, for short-hand purposes, may be denom-~~

~~inated~~ sports medicine. ~~Our inquiries revealed that~~

while ~~there is recognition~~ _people recognize_ ~~of the~~ _as a_ growing problem ~~of~~

(injuries and drug abuse) in sports, ~~and in this instance~~

~~the problem is common to~~ amateur as well as profes-

sional ~~sports,~~ ~~there appears to be little systematic~~ _no one has discovered how_

~~study of the means and methods~~ to prevent ~~sports~~ in-

juries or ~~to~~ understand ~~the effects of~~ _how_ drugs ~~on~~ _affect_ athletes

and ~~to educate the profession on the proper use of~~ _should be prescribed -- or proscribed -- for_

them.

~~drugs.~~

Prose like this gives you no help in deciding what is _impor-tant_, central to the assertion. Here the main villain is the absence of an actor—no clear kicker and hence blocked kick and kickee. Look at what getting rid of the basic sludge does to sentence shape:

REVISION

Sports medicine. Our investigation of player safety exposed a larger problem—sports medicine. While people recognize injuries and drugs as a growing prob-lem in sports, amateur as well as professional, no one has discovered how to prevent injuries or understood how drugs affect athletes and should be prescribed—or proscribed—for them. (52 words—LF 47%)

We've cut the passage in half but, more important, we've given it a shape the voice can enjoy. By tightening up the first sentence, we've brought "player safety" and "a larger problem" into close juxtaposition, so that the second seems to emerge from the first with more naturalness. And the appositive "—sports medicine" explains what the "larger problem" is with a puff of energy. A quick series the eye can follow: investigation . . . larger problem . . . sports medicine. And the second sentence now allows its main components to be seen at a glance:

— people recognize injuries as a growing problem
— no one has discovered how to prevent injuries
— no one has understood how drugs affect athletes.

I've added a kind of visual pun on "pre-scribed" and "pro-scribed" at the end. It may seem a little cutesy but it *focuses* the drug problem—use OK, abuse not OK—in the very *appearance* of the words. Shape here helps both eye and ear in the most immediate kind of way and help like this the naturally shapeless Official Style always needs.

CHAPTER THREE

Sentence Length, Rhythm, and Sound

Take a piece of your prose and a red pencil and draw a slash after every sentence. Two or three pages ought to make a large enough sample. If the red marks occur at regular intervals, you have, as they used to say in the White House, a problem. You can chart the problem another way, if you like. Choose a standard length for one sentence and then do a bar-graph. If it looks like this,

    ————
    ————
    ————
    —————
    ——————
    ——

dandy. If like this,

    ————
    ————
    ————
    ————
    ————

not so dandy. Obviously, no absolute quantitative standards exist for how much variety is good, how little bad, but the principle couldn't be easier. Vary sentence length. Naturally enough, complex patterns will fall into long sentences and emphatic conclusions work well when short. But no general rule prevails except to avoid monotony. When you think about sentence length in a *particular* case, of course, all the other concomitant variables of style enter in since they determine sentence length to begin with. You can't revise a passage *only* to vary sentence length. In fact, a varied pattern usually reflects other stylistic choices already made, rather than being an end in itself; it represents a relative virtue not an absolute one, an appearance of health rather than a vital sign.

We can now add one last rule to the PM:

1. Circle the prepositions.
2. Circle the "is" forms.
3. Ask "Who is kicking Who?"
4. Put this "kicking" action in a simple (not compound) active verb.
5. Start fast—no mindless introductions.
6. Write out each sentence on a blank sheet of paper and mark off its basic rhythmic units with a "/".
7. Read the passage aloud with emphasis and feeling.
8. Mark off sentence lengths in the passage with a "/".

Here's how it *should* be done, a model report of scientific research. The passage comes from Horace Judson's account of the discovery of the double-helix structure of DNA (see how easy it is to fall into an "of" string?) in his history of modern biology, *The Eighth Day of Creation:*

Compared with all previous B patterns that Franklin had obtained, these two pictures were vivid, No. 51 especially so. The overall pattern was a huge blurry diamond. The top and bottom points of the diamond were capped by heavily exposed, dark arcs. From the bulls-eye, a striking arrangement of short, horizontal smears stepped out along the diagonals in the shape of an X or a maltese cross. The pattern shouted helix.

The paragraph charts out like this; the last sentence short and emphatic, its last word climactic:

19 _____
 8 _____
15 _____
26 _____
 4 _____

And not only the last sentence but all the sentences end strongly. And the varied sentence lengths seem to echo the stages of causality the passage seeks to describe. Read the passage aloud a time or two, to fix the rhythm in your mind. Then read this:

Each person to whom this notice is addressed is entitled to submit, or request the Department of Labor to submit, to the District Director described above a comment on the question of whether the Plan meets the requirements of the Internal Revenue Code of 1954. Two or more such persons may join in a single comment or request. If such a person or persons request the Department of Labor to submit a comment and that department declines to do so in respect of one or more matters raised in the request, the person or persons so requesting may submit a comment to the District Director in respect of the matters on which the Department of Labor declines to comment. A comment submitted to the District Director must be received by him on or before November 4, 1978.

However, if it is being submitted on a matter on which the Department of Labor was first requested, but declined to comment, the comment must be received by the District Director on or before the later of November 4, 1978 or the 15th day after the day on which the Department of Labor notifies such person or persons that it declines to comment, but in no event later than November 19, 1978. A request of the Department of Labor to submit a comment must be received by that department on or before October 15, 1978, or if the person or persons making the request wish to preserve their right to submit a comment to the District Director in the event the Department of Labor declines to comment, on or before October 5, 1978.

45 _____

13 _____

61 _____

17 _____

81 _____

60 _____

Shows us, for a start, that varying sentence length by itself doesn't guarantee much. Graphing length here tells you that almost all your sentences are too long, but it can't do more than suggest the main problem — length has no relation to meaning. The eye can't help the sense. Nor can the ear. Sentences like these have neither shape nor rhythm. They are simply sawed off in convenient lengths, like wallboard. The voice has no place to go in re-creating them. To the inner ear which voices prose to ourselves they are literally unreadable. No rules prevail for prose rhythm but one intuitive guide stands ready for us all. Voice. If prose is hard to read aloud, it will be hard to read silently. If it offers the voice no guidance, does not invite it to stress this and elide that, to rise and fall in pitch, then it is going to be hard to follow.

Let's work through a sentence or two of this wallboard prose to make the point:

> Each person to whom this notice is addressed is entitled to submit, or request the Department of Labor to submit, to the District Director described above a comment on the question of whether the Plan meets the requirements of the Internal Revenue Code of 1954. (45)

People writing everyday prose under pressure seldom have time to polish, but anyone can do this kind of quick simonize. What comes out allows the voice at least a couple of accents:

> You can tell the District Director, or ask the Labor Department to tell him, how the Plan compares to the Internal Revenue Code of 1954. (25)

A shape of sorts:

1. You can tell him
2. or ask the Labor Department to tell him
3. how the Plan fits IRS

If (1) or (2), then (3). Form follows function. And a LF of 44%.

One more:

> If such a person or persons request the Department of Labor to submit a comment and that Department declines to do so in respect of one or more matters raised in the request, the person or persons so re-

questing may submit a comment to the District Director in respect of the matters on which the Department of Labor declines to comment. (30)

Putting this pseudo-legalistic guff into English:

Whenever you ask the Labor Department to comment and they decline, you can write the District Director yourself. (18)

Notice how the voice wants to rise on "Labor," "comment," and "decline" and on "you" and "yourself"? The idea comes in through your ears: "Whenever X, then Y." And a LF of 40%.

The elements of prose style—grammar, syntax, shape, rhythm, emphasis, level of usage and so on—all work as dependent variables. Change one and you change the rest. But of them all, rhythm constitutes the most vital of prose's vital life-signs. Rhythmless, unemphatic prose always indicates that something has gone wrong. And Tin Ears, insensitivity to the sound of words, indicate that the hearing which registers rhythm has been turned off.

Tin Ears have become so common that often you can't tell mistakes from intentions. An advertising flack for the Army writes:

Like any new departure in motivating men, the path to a Modern Volunteer Army is beset with perils and pitfalls but it also has potential for progress.

Is the alliteration of "*m*otivating *m*en," "*p*erils and *p*itfalls," "*p*otential for *p*rogress" intended or accidental? It works, at all events, obvious though it may be. The three central phrases of the sentence are spotlighted by an alliterated pair of words, and the last two pairs are put into almost visual contrast:

> perils and pitfalls
> potential for progress

And "motivating men" finds an alliterative echo in "Modern" while the *p* alliteration has a pre-echo in "path." All this seems to indicate premeditation and a heavy hand. But the writer obviously creates a specific shape and rhythm. Not so in the following sentence from a guide to practical workaday writing:

> For the writer the practice of bad writing is harmful, for it results in an inhibition of his responses to intellectual and imaginative stimuli.

Notice the "*in an in*hibition" sequence, forcing the reader to babble? And did the writer see the "harm*ful for*" doublet? Notice how it works against his purpose here? The punctuation encourages us to stop after "harmful" while the *ful–for* alliterative couplet wants us to rush on without a stop. And he has another mouthful-of-peanut-butter *n–m* cluster in "respo*n*ses to i*n*tellectual and i*m*ag-i*n*ative sti*m*uli." I've deliberately chosen an example where this unspeakable cluster did *not* stand out, just to show how often one is there, nevertheless. Prose will always possess a spoken dimension so long as we continue to speak. If we ignore it, it will not go away; it will come back to plague us. How to fix this example? First, the standard drill. Circle the prepositions. Get rid of "is." Ask Who is kicking Who. Squeeze out the lard. Here is the original again:

> For the writer, the practice of bad writing is harmful,

for it results in an inhibition of his responses to intellectual and imaginative stimuli.

The actor is "bad writing" and the action lies buried in
"inhibition." So: "Bad writing inhibits a writer's intellect
and imagination." (LF 66%) "The practice of" is one of
those "the fact that" fillers. "Results in an inhibition of"
is one of those "is" + noun + preposition substitutions
for the simple verb "inhibits," like "stands in violation of"
for "violates." "Harmful" is implied by "inhibits."
"Responses to intellectual and imaginative stimuli,"
means simply "intellect and imagination." And so we
have "Bad writing inhibits a writer's intellect and imagination." And, since our subject is Tin Ears, we notice
right away that "mind" instead of "intellect" smooths out
that *intellect* and *imagination* cluster of *m*'s, *n*'s, and *t*'s.
"Bad writing inhibits a writer's mind and imagination."
We've also substituted a single-syllable word for a three-
syllable word, and this helps out in a sentence already
overloaded with two- and three-syllable words. Notice
how they monotonize the rhythm?
   What has happened here? We've revised the sentence
with our do-it-yourself PM and the rhythmless morass has
taken care of itself. Interdependent variables, again. Find
out Who is kicking Who, and the problems that fan out
from this central misapprehension may solve themselves.
Let's mark the original sentence for rhythm. I'll put a
slash for each cadence:

> For the writer / the practice / of bad writing / is
> harmful / for it results / in an inhibition / of his
> responses / to intellectual / and imaginative /
> stimuli.

Every unit runs to almost the same length—da-da-dum,

da-da-dum. You can see how the prepositional phrases, strung out like a snake's vertebrae, prohibit any life or vigor. The revision, while not yet "Shall I compare thee to a summer's day," at least has components of different sizes:

> Bad writing / inhibits a writer's mind / and imagination.

The stress falls naturally at the end, where we want it, on "mind" and "imagination." (What would happen to this concluding stress if we said "mind and heart" instead? Would it make the concluding rhythmic unit better or worse?)

Squeezing the lard out of prose seems sometimes to liberate a natural rhythm, modest but clear, that was waiting to be freed. Look at this before-and-after nugget of business reporting:

> BEFORE: Whereas the President emerges more as a victor, the Chairman seems defeated.
>
> AFTER: The President seems to win, the Chairman to lose.

A lard factor of 25% obscures the natural modest stress on "wins" and "loses." Often rhythmic emphasis, once we are sensitive to it, will tell us what to pare away. Consider this example:

> We are not surprised or shocked by her story or the manner in which she tells it.

First, *s*urprised and *s*hocked and *s*tory ring a faint alarm bell. We don't really need both verbs, since shock implies surprise. And we want the shape and rhythm of the sentence to underline the opposition of story and telling. So:

> We are shocked neither by her story nor how she tells it.

"Neither . . . nor" sets up a natural contrasting rhythm, provided we keep the contrasted elements short and close together.

Often a long string of one-syllable words will break up the rhythm as here:

> The Director's overwhelming presence in relation *to that of the rest of the* employees strikes us immediately.

Seven one-syllable words in a row dulls the prose bite as well as a string of jawbreakers does. Again, the villain is that string of prepositional phrases. The fix simply lines up kicker, kicking and kickee: "The Director, obviously, overwhelms the other employees." (Do you see the similarity, within the sentence, to the problem of varying length from sentence to sentence?) Once your ears have had their consciousness raised, they'll catch the easy sound problems as they flow from the pen—"however clever" will become "however shrewd" in the first draft—and the harder ones will seem easier to revise.

Here, preserved in a lump of sociologese, is a pair of ears whose consciousness badly needs raising. Try reading the passage aloud and with emphasis. Act as if the passage really said something important (what would happen to the sound if I had written "significant" here, instead of "important"?).

> Having shown the applicability of analysis of covariance in straightforward research situations, I

shall go on to indicate how several other important methodological topics can be profitably conceptualized as isomorphic in logical structure to the general linear model. . . . For several other topics as well, notably the ecological correlation fallacy, the study of compositional effects, the construction of a "standardized" index, and even the percentaging of cross tables, the logic of linear models is useful. . . .

In regression analysis, as in analysis of variance, if the normality of errors assumption is made, one can analyze the variance due to the explanatory variables, ascertain its significance, and proceed in the same manner as indicated for the analysis of variance situation, and can also test hypotheses about specific values of the parameters.

Reading something like this with emphasis gives you the giggles. You cannot revise what you cannot understand, and I do not understand this. Maybe the subject simply repels any shape or rhythm. Maybe the jargon *is* the meaning. If the author had written, "Having shown how covariance analysis fits straightforward research problems," maybe scientific rigor would have been compromised. But whatever it means, your prose ought not read like a laundry list. Prose like this has become generally unreadable, has lost a whole dimension of expressibility. Notice how many polysyllabic words he uses: *applicability, analysis, covariance, straightforward, methodological, profitably, conceptualized, isomorphic, ecological correlation fallacy*. And the sentences are all about the same length.

Revising a passage in The Official Style for shape and emphasis often means only taking out the stuffing. The rhythm then comes almost of itself. Here's an easy piece of educationese from — of all things — a writing textbook.

ORIGINAL

The workbook *Advanced Reading and Composition Skills* is intended for use with college students who are studying English as a first or second language. The Supplemental Activities following each of the 10 lessons in the text may thus be appropriately adapted by the instructor for use with native speakers of English or with students who are studying English as a second language or dialect. The purpose of the text is to acquaint students with three reading techniques to be used for specific reading purposes. Seventy reading selections are provided for practicing the reading techniques; numerous suggestions are given for composition topics, listening comprehension, and analysis and discussion activities stemming from and enlarging upon topics presented in the lessons.

REVISION

~~The workbook~~ *Advanced Reading and Composition*

Skills (is) intended for ~~use with~~ college students ~~who are~~

studying English as a first or second language. The

Supplemental Activities following each ~~of the 10~~

lesson**s** ~~in the text~~ may ~~thus~~ be ~~appropriately~~ adapted

~~by the instructor~~ for ~~use with~~ native speakers, ~~of~~ second-

dialect speakers,   foreigners.
 ̖~~English~~ or ~~with students who are studying English as a~~

~~second language or dialect.~~ The ~~purpose of the~~ text ~~is~~

~~to~~ acquaint**s** students with three reading techniques ~~to~~ and

provides
~~be used for~~ (specific) ~~reading purposes.~~ Seventy reading

selections ~~are provided~~ for practicing ~~the reading~~ them.
~~techniques; numerous~~ It suggestion~~s~~ ~~are given for~~ composition and ~~(topics)~~ listening comprehension, and ~~analysis~~ further
~~and~~ discussion~~s~~ ~~activities stemming from and enlarg-~~
~~ing upon~~ of the ~~(topics)~~ ~~presented in the~~ lesson~~s~~

How does it look when revised?

> *Advanced Reading and Composition Skills* is in-
> tended for college students studying English as a first
> or second language. The Supplemental Activities
> following each lesson may be adapted for native
> speakers, second-dialect speakers, or foreigners. The
> text acquaints students with three specific reading
> techniques and provides seventy reading selections for
> practicing them. It suggests composition and listening
> comprehension topics and further discussions of the
> lesson topics. (LF 44%)

This kind of revision is dead easy and no author can ex-
cuse himself for not doing it. People often say that prose
in the workaday world often must be written when there
isn't time for this kind of revision. But it's easy there too.
If you practice doing it, you won't write this way to begin
with. The Official Style is no *fun* to write but it isn't easy,
either. Rhythm and shape make things easier, not
harder, and for all concerned.

When you try to write rhythmical prose, you are in-
viting your reader to perform. Prose varies in how this invitation is extended. Some prose, our wallboard prose for
example, offers no guidance at all. Sometimes we're given

some performance instructions, taken partway on stage.
Let's look, for variety, at a most *un*official style which
does this. A Los Angeles guru, the central character in
Lewis Yablonsky's wonderful *The Hippie Trip*, is com-
menting on the Big Sur hippie scene:

> —When I first got up there, it was a real romantic
> kind of picture. Man, it was kind of foggy. There were
> those really beautiful people—men, women, kids, dogs
> and cats, and campfires. It seemed quiet and stable.
> And I really felt like love was about me. I thought,
> "This is the place, man. It was happening. . . . I don't
> have to do it. I would just fit in and do my thing and
> that would be like a groove."
>
> After we were there about fifteen or twenty
> minutes, I heard the people bitching and moaning. I
> listened to it for a while and circulated around to hear
> more about it and, man, I couldn't believe it. Here
> they were secure in their land—beautiful land, where
> they could be free—and all these people were doing
> was bitching and moaning. I thought, "Oh, shit,
> man! Do I have to go into this kind of shit again where
> I gotta step in and get heavy and get ratty and get
> people to start talking? Do I have to get them to be
> open and get in some dialogue and get some com-
> munication going and organization? What the . . . . . is
> wrong with the leadership here, that this kind of state
> of affairs is happening? And why do I have to do it
> again? Man, I'm through with it. I just got through
> with hepatitis and double pneumonia and . . . .
> it!" Then I really felt bad.

This is speech, for a start. And hippie speech, heavily syncopated speech, sliding quickly over interim syllables from
heavy stress to heavy stress: "first," "romantic," "foggy,"

"really," "love." Once you know the syncopated pattern, it is easy to mark up a passage like this. But if you don't know the pattern? Imagine yourself a foreigner trying to read this passage with a natural emphasis. It does sometimes give clues. "This is the *place, man. It was happening. I* don't have to do it." The arrangement of the words underscores the sense—the scene has become the actor and the actor the scene. So, too, the alliterative repetition of "go into," "gotta step in," "get heavy," "get ratty," "get people" gives us a clear performance clue. But the passage by itself does not include a full guide to its performance.

How *can* prose include such a guide? Traditionally, it has done so most often by patterns of repetition, balance, antithesis, and parallelism. As a contrast to the guru prose, consider this very old-fashioned example of an Official Style. It was written by Lord Brougham (1778–1868), a famous Parliamentary orator, who defended Queen Caroline in the divorce proceedings George IV had brought against her. This kind of Official Style seems fulsome to us, but notice how many performance clues it contains:

But, my lords, I am not reduced to this painful necessity. I feel that if I were to touch this branch of the case now, until any event shall afterwards show that unhappily I am deceiving myself—I feel that if I were now to approach the great subject of recrimination, I should seem to give up the higher ground of innocence on which I rest my cause; I should seem to be justifying when I plead Not Guilty; I should seem to argue in extenuation and in palliation of offences, or levities, or improprieties, the least and the lightest of which I stand here utterly to deny.

Several powerful variables contend in a prose like this. The patterning aims above all to establish a tone of high seriousness. But look at it simply for performance clues. It includes precisely the performance dimension that modern official prose lacks. It is written to be performed and tells us exactly how it ought to be performed. Shape and sound coincide. It builds to a climactic central assertion and then tapers off. Perhaps a diagram will help:

> But, my lords,
> I am not reduced to this painful necessity.
> I feel that if
> I were to touch this branch of the case now, until any
>   event shall afterwards show that unhappily
> I am deceiving myself —
> I feel that if
> I were now to approach the great subject of
>   recrimination,
> I should seem to give up the higher ground of
>   innocence on which
> I rest my cause;
>   I should seem to be justifying when
>   I plead Not Guilty;
>   I should seem to argue in extenuation
>   and in palliation of
>   offences, levities, or improprieties,
>   the least and the lightest of which
>   I stand here utterly to deny.

We don't write like this anymore, but perhaps we should, at least a little. Official prose seldom is declaimed nowadays, to be sure. But when declamation goes out of official prose entirely, the life goes out of it, too. For declamation is an affair of sight and sound patterns and ignoring these, as we have been seeing, drains the life out of prose, slows it down, blurs its focus. To ignore the kind of training which produced Brougham's style, training in the shape, rhythm, and emphasis of the sentence, leads inevitably to our characteristic modern Official Style. Whether you relish Brougham's style, as I do, or find it a trifle fulsome, you ought to try in your own prose to give equally good performance instructions. For, again, that is what sentence rhythm is — a series of instructions for how your sentence should be performed.

Americans though, have always found attention to verbal performance embarrassing and affected. We almost never listen to ourselves talk. No corrective voice feedback at all. And we ignore our speech for the same reason that we despise "style" in writing. Words don't matter. Only the idea. Americans have always been natural romantics. Natural is best. Premeditated speech has to be somehow insincere speech. Snobbish. Undemocratic. Fake. We've grown, as a result, into a nation of Tin Ears. Without trying to solve the paradox that only artifice is natural to man, surely the therapy is simply to listen.

CHAPTER FOUR

The Official Style

Up to now we've been analyzing particular stylistic elements — shape, rhythm, emphasis. We've seen, in the process, that these elements are interrelated, that they seem to proceed from the same aesthetic, constitute a common style. In the examples we've been revising, we've been in effect translating from The Official Style into plain English. Now we are going to do this directly, focus on The Official Style as an exercise in stylistic analysis and translation. At the same time, we'll try, instead of simply condemning The Official Style, to ask how and why it has come about, how it works in the world.

Students of style have traditionally distinguished three basic levels — high, middle, low. The content of these categories varied somewhat, but usually the high style was a formal and ornamental style for a solemn and ritualized occasion, the low style enshrined the loose and sloppy intercourse of daily life, and the middle style stood somewhere in between. Since World War II, American prose has worked a pronounced variation on this enduring pattern. The low style has pretty much disintegrated into a series of "I-mean-like-you-know" shrugs and spastic tics, like, you know? And as we have come to suspect fancy language and formal ceremony as undemocratic, we have come to suspect the high style, too. As a substitute, we've clasped to our bosoms The Official Style — a style which is formal without ever pretending to be grand. The Official Style is often stigmatized as bureaucratese or jargon and often is both. But it is a genuine style, and one that reflects the genuine bureaucratization of American life. It has its own rules and its own ambitions, and anyone writing in business or government nowadays in America must come to know both. The Official Style comes to us in two main guises, as the language of social science and as the language of bureaucracy. Social science wants above all to sound scientific — disinterested, impersonal, factual. Bureaucracy wants above all to sound official — neutral, formal, authoritative, inevitable. Both ambitions converge on a common set of verbal habits, The Official Style.

The Official Style runs from school days to retirement. As soon as you realize that you live "in a system," whether P.S. 41, the University of California, the Department of Agriculture, or General Motors, you start developing The Official Style. Used unthinkingly, it provides the quickest tip-off that you have become system-sick and look at life only through the system's eyes. It is a scribal style, ritualized, formulaic, using a special vocabulary to describe a special kind of world, the world of bureaucratic officialdom. And it is, increasingly, the only kind of prose style America ever sees. It is also, along with the social changes that sponsor it, the main reason for our prose problem. The low style has dissolved, the high style has hardened and dehydrated, and the middle style has simply evaporated. The Official Style threatens to replace all three.

If you can analyze, write, and translate it, maybe you can find your niche in The System — public sector or private — without losing your soul to it. For you may have to write in The Official Style but you don't have to think in it. If you are the first on the scene after the sports car has missed the curve, climbed the hedge, and ended up on the lawn, you won't ask the driver, as did one policeman, "How, uh, sir, did you achieve this configuration?"

Sometimes you can see The Official Style seizing its prey like a boa constrictor and gradually squeezing the life out of it. Here's a college student first feeling its grip.

> Twelve-year-old boys like to fight. Consequently, on several occasions I explained to them the negative aspects of fighting. Other responsibilities included keeping them dry (when near the creek or at times of rain), seeing that they bathed, attending to any minor wounds they acquired, and controlling their mischievous behavior. Another responsibility was remaining patient with the children.

The first sentence says simply what it has to say. The second sentence starts to sound like a report. It strives for a needless explicitness ("on several occasions") and it aims for a pseudoscientific neutrality of description, "the negative aspects of fighting." To remain on the same stylistic level as the first sentence, it ought to read, "So, I often told them to stop." "Other responsibilities included" is the language of a job description. The frantic scramble of a summer camp is being viewed through a personnel form. The prose is scary as well as stilted because life has been reduced to something that will fit in a file cabinet. Only on official forms do small boys "acquire minor wounds" or counselors "attend" them. In life, they cut themselves and you give them a Band-Aid. In life, you keep them out of the creek and out of the rain, instead of "keeping them dry (when near the creek or at times of rain)." And, instead of "controlling their mischievous behavior," you make them behave or even give them a kick in the pants. As for "Another respons-

ibility was remaining patient with children," that trans-
lates into, "I had to keep my temper." If the writer had
stayed on the low-style level he began with, he would have
written:

> Twelve-year-old boys like to fight. Often, I had to
> stop them. And I had to keep them out of the rain,
> and the creek, and mischief generally. I had to give
> out Band-Aids and keep my temper.

Why didn't he? You don't write The Official Style by
nature. It has to be learned. Why did he fall into it here?
He was applying for something. And you apply for something—in this case, admission to medical school—on a
form. And a form requires an official style. The Official
Style. It makes what you've done sound important and,
still more important than important, *official*.

Ever since George Orwell's famous essay "Politics and
the English Language" (1946), The Official Style has
been interpreted as a vast conspiracy to soften our minds
and corrupt our political judgment. Social science jargon
has been seen as pure hokum, an attempt to seem more
scientific than you are. And the language of the Pentagon
and Dow Chemical bureaucrats during the Vietnam War
often seemed to combine the worst of these two worlds.
The Orwell conspiracy theory is sometimes true, but not
the whole truth. We all want to fit in, to talk the language
of the country. This desire is what keeps society glued
together. So the impulses that attract us to The Official
Style are not always perverse or depraved. Just the opposite. They are the primary social impulses. And so
when we analyze The Official Style, we're really talking
about how we live now, about our *society* as well as our
prose, about how to survive in The System. What does the
prose tell us about the society?

Well, it is a euphemistic society, for a start. It thinks of every town dump as a "Sanitary Landfill Site," every mentally retarded child as "exceptional," every dog catcher as an "animal welfare officer," every pig pen as a "unitary hog-raising facility." Society may have its pains and problems, but language can sugarcoat them. An official stylist would never say that an area was so polluted plants obviously couldn't grow there. Instead: "Natural biotic habitats are conspicuously absent from the region."

The second rule in this society is "Keep your head down. Don't assert anything you'll have to take the blame for. Don't, if you can help it, assert anything at all." Anthony Sampson, in his *Anatomy of Britain*, has culled a few examples of this supercaution from a British Civil Service version of The Official Style and supplied plain language translations.

We hope that it is fully appreciated that . . .
   You completely fail to realize that . . .

Greater emphasis should be laid on . . .
   You haven't bothered to notice . . .

We have the impression that insufficient study has been given to . . .
   No one has considered . . .

Our enquiry seemed to provide a welcome opportunity for discussions of problems of this kind . . .
   No one had thought of that before . . .

We do not think that there is sufficient awareness . . .
   There is ignorance . . .

There has been a tendency in the past to overestimate the possibilities of useful short-term action in public investment . . .
   You should look ahead . . .

> There should be an improvement in the arrangements
> to enable ministers to discharge their collective
> responsibility . . .
>   The cabinet should work together . . .

The main rule is clear. Don't make an assertion you can get tagged with later. It may come back to haunt you. So never write "I think" or "I did." Keep the verbs passive and impersonal: "It was concluded that" or "appropriate action was initiated on the basis of systematic discussion indicating that." Often, as with politicians being interviewed on TV, The Official Style aims deliberately at saying nothing at all, but saying it in the required way. Or at saying the obvious in a seemingly impressive way. The Official Stylist must seem in control of everything but responsible for nothing. Thus a congressman, instead of saying that the government will listen to consumer complaints, says that it will "review existing mechanisms of consumer input, thruput, and output and seek ways of improving these linkages via consumer consumption channels." The computer language of input, output, and interface has been seized upon by The Official Style as a kind of poetic diction, a body of sacred and intrinsically beautiful metaphors. Thus, a U.S. senator indicted on bribery charges does not ask the advice of his friends. Instead, bathing in computer charisma, he is "currently receiving personal and political input from my supporters and friends throughout the state."

It is often hard to tell with The Official Style how much is self-conscious put-on and how much real ineptitude, genuine system-sickness. Students often say that the length and physical weight of their papers is more important than what they say, yet it is not only in school that papers are graded thus. Here is a famous Washington lawyer, talking about legal language.

In these days when every other type of professional report, good or poor, is dressed up in a lovely ringed and colored plastic binder, some people still are prone to judge legal performance quantitatively by verbal volume. Thirty years ago two of us answered a difficult and intricate legal problem by concisely writing: "Gentlemen, after examining the statute in your state, all analogous statutes, and all of the cases, we have concluded that what you want to do is lawful." That client was not happy; he went down to Wall Street, got the same opinion backed by thirty turgid typewritten pages, and felt much more comfortable. (Quoted in Joseph C. Guelden's *The Superlawyers*)

It is not only bureaucrats who find length and obscurity impressive.

Here is another example of The Official Style inflating something short and sweet:

A policy decision inexorably enforced upon a depression-prone individual whose posture in respect to his total psychophysical environment is rendered antagonistic by apprehension or by inner-motivated disinclination for ongoing participation in human existence is the necessity for effectuating a positive selection between two alternative programs of action, namely, (a) the continuance of the above-mentioned existence irrespective of the dislocations, dissatisfactions, and disabilities incurred in such a mode, or (b) the voluntary termination of such existence by self-initiated instrumentality, irrespective in this instance of the undetermined character of the subsequent environment, if any, in which the subject may be positioned as an end result of this irrevocable determination.

Serious or a joke? A joke. In fact, one of the clever varia-
tions on common clichés devised by Richard D. Altick in
his *A Preface to Critical Reading* to illustrate The Official
Style. The text varied is, of course, "To be or not be, that
is the question."

Now, by contrast, someone genuinely system-sick. No
joke. He has come to *think* in The Official Style. The
librarian of a large library, in a very large bureaucracy, is
trying to tell us that some books will be kept behind the
desk, others put on shelves outside:

> Primarily, this reorganization and the related
> changes are designed to facilitate the processing of
> lists. Placing responsibility for the processing of lists
> directly within the Technical Processing Division will
> provide a smoother and more efficient work flow,
> which we anticipate will result in your materials
> becoming more readily available. Second, it will allow
> optimum access to the collection, and third, provide a
> browsing capability formerly denied users of reserved
> materials.
>
> For this new system to be successful we need your
> full cooperation. The attached Guidelines for Reserve
> Lists details the manner in which we need lists pre-
> pared. Essentially, we are requesting that required
> readings be distinguished from optional readings. Re-
> quired readings stipulated for two hour use will be
> placed on closed reserve in an area behind the cir-
> culation desk. Required readings circulating for one
> day will remain in the open stacks; however, as op-
> posed to regular open stack materials, these books will
> be marked to indicate one day use. Optional readings
> will circulate for regular loan periods.
>
> In the past, the primary means for soliciting
> faculty input for acquiring materials for the College
> Library has been through reserve lists. It is our desire

that optimal reading lists for undergraduates will be an effective mechanism for faculty to identify materials for the library's open stack collection.

It is our hope that you will find these changes mutually beneficial for yourselves and your students.

Your cooperation and assistance in this matter will be greatly appreciated.

If he translated this into language less wordy, shapeless, pompous, and pretentious, he might make things clearer to the faculty but he would be only a librarian, not a bureaucratic witch doctor. He would be simply putting the books out on the shelf, not "providing a browsing capability." Try a revision of your own in this spirit.

You must, if you are to write prose in an America and a world fated to become ever more bureaucratic, learn how to use The Official Style, even perhaps how to enjoy it, without becoming imprisoned by it. You must manage to remember who is on first base, even if often you will not want to let on that you know.

Long ago, La Rochefoucauld talked about a grave manner as "a mysterious carriage of the body to cover defects of the mind." The Official Style has elevated this into an article of faith. Here is a sociological sample collected by Malcolm Cowley, with his translation:

In effect, it was hypothesized that certain physical data categories including housing types and densities, land use characteristics, and ecological location constitute a scalable content area. This could be called a continuum of residential desirability. Likewise, it was hypothesized that several social data categories, describing the same census tracts, and referring generally to the social stratification system of the city, would also be scalable. This scale would be called a continuum of socio-economic status. Thirdly, it was hypothesized that there would be a high positive correlation between the scale types on each continuum.

Here's the translation:

Rich people live in big houses set further apart than those of poor people. By looking at an aerial photograph of any American city, we can distinguish the richer from the poorer neighborhoods. ("Sociological Habit Patterns in Linguistic Transmogrification," *The Reporter*, September 20, 1956)

Such prose seems to aim at being scientific but actually wants to be priestly, to cast a witch doctor's spell. To translate the prose into a plain style—that is, to revise it into ordinary English—breaks the spell and defeats the purpose.

We face, then, the euphemistic habit yet again, though on a larger scale. The Official Style always wants to make things seem better than they are, more mysterious and yet somehow more controlled, more inevitable. It strives, at all times, both to disarm and to impress us. It suggests that it sees the world differently—sees, even, a different world. It suggests that those who see in this way form a happy band of brothers. Now such a use of language does not, to students of literature, sound unfamiliar. It is called poetic diction. And this is what The Official Style amounts to—a kind of poetic diction. Here we come to the central problem with The Official Style. There is no point in reproaching it for not being clear. It does not really want to be clear. It wants to be *poetic*. At its best, it wants to tell you how it *feels* to be an official, to project the sense of numinous self-importance officialdom confers. It wants to make a prosaic world mysterious.

I know, I know. It doesn't do it very well. But that's not the point. Until we see what it is trying to do, we can neither understand it nor translate it with any pleasure. Maybe a comparison from another time and context will make the point clearer. Here is a series of plain language translations of Official Style poetic diction which the English poet Alexander Pope compiled for a satire on false poetic sublimity called *Peri Bathos* (1728). He gives first the poetic diction and then the ordinary language equivalent.

POETIC DICTION	PLAIN ENGLISH
For whom thus rudely pleads my loud-tongued gate That he may enter?. . .	Who knocks at the Door?
Advance the fringed curtains of thy eyes, And tell me who comes yonder . . .	See who is there.
The wooden guardian of our privacy Quick on its axle turn . . .	Shut the Door.
Bring me what Nature, tailor to the *Bear* To *Man* himself denied: She gave me Cold But would not give me Clothes . . .	Bring my Clothes.

Bring forth some remnant of
   the *Promethean* theft,
Quick to expand th'
   inclement air congealed
By *Boreas'* rude breath . . .   Light the Fire.

Yon Luminary amputation
   needs,
Thus shall you save its half-
   extinguished life.   Snuff the Candle.

Apply thine engine to the
   spongy door,
Set *Bacchus* from his glassy
   prison free,
And strip white *Ceres* of her   Uncork the Bottle,
   nut-brown coat.   and cut the Bread.

And here is a modern version of such a list, culled from
an Environmental Impact Statement filed by the FAA.

POETIC DICTION	PLAIN ENGLISH
"limited in length"	short
"small faunal species"	rats
"experience growth"	grow
"annoyance factors"	annoyances
"police protection services"	police
"aircraft with lower noise emission characteristics"	quieter planes
"overlain by impervious surfaces"	paved
"exotic effluents"	chemicals
"weedy species"	weeds
"stepwise methodology"	method

"pollutant emissions control
   strategies"   smog filters
"olfactory impact"   smell

Here is yet another glossary, an unintentional self-satire
this time, issued by the U.S. Office of Education (1971).

POETIC DICTION	PLAIN ENGLISH
Allocation of personnel and logistic resources to accomplish an identifiable objective. Activities constitute the basis for defining personnel assignments and for scheduling system operations.	Activity
The splitting of an entity into its constituent parts and the determination of relations among the parts and groups of the components.	Analysis
Production and refinement of a system or a product through trial-revision until it accomplishes its specified objectives.	Development
Those things (actions) that must be done to accomplish the overall job are referred to as functions.	Functions
To carry out. To fulfill. To give practical effect to and ensure of actual fulfillment by concrete measures.	Implement
Enhanced performance on any important dimension without	Improvement

detriment to the other essential dimensions.

The job to be done, be it a product, a completed service, or a change in the condition of something or somebody.

Mission

A discrepancy or differential between "what is" and "what should be" (i.e., "what is required" or "what is desired"). In educational planning, "need" refers to problems rather than solutions, to the student "product" rather than to the resources for achieving that product, to the ends of education rather than to the means for attaining those ends.

Need

That toward which effort is directed. An intent statement and production for which a procedure is developed and resources allocated with a specific time frame and a measurable product signaling attainment.

Objectives

The organizational, procedural, technological, and support arrangements by which an agency has the capacity to apply problem-solving processes to any problem that it may face.

Planning Capability or Planning Competence

Elements of a function that, when performed by people and things in proper sequential order, will or should resolve the parent function. Tasks may be performed by people, equipment, or people/equipment combination.	Tasks

(Robert A. Watson, "Making Things Perfectly Clear," *Saturday Review*, July 24, 1971).

This bureaucratic glossary was issued in the name of clarity but aims obviously at something else entirely, at a playful, poetic, ornamental use of language. Those who use The Official Style seldom acknowledge the paradox, but you must learn to see it if you are not to make grotesque mistakes. Clarity is often the last thing The Official Style really wants to create and, if you find yourself in a bureaucratic context, often the last thing *you* want to create. If you are writing a government memo, a sociological report, or a grant proposal in education, writing it in plain English could be disastrous. You may well want, in marshaling your thoughts, to write out an ordinary-language version. But you must then translate it into The Official Style. You must, that is, learn to read, write, and translate The Official Style as if it were a foreign language. Play games with it by all means, but don't get fooled by it.

Bureaucrats have, in the last few years, begun to do just this—play games with it. One government official, Philip Broughton, created something called the "Systematic Buzz Phrase Projector." It consists of three columns of words:

Column 1	Column 2	Column 3
0. integrated	0. management	0. options
1. total	1. organizational	1. flexibility
2. systematized	2. monitored	2. capability
3. parallel	3. reciprocal	3. mobility
4. functional	4. digital	4. programming
5. responsive	5. logistical	5. concept
6. optional	6. transitional	6. time-phase
7. synchronized	7. incremental	7. projection
8. compatible	8. third-generation	8. hardware
9. balanced	9. policy	9. contingency

(*Newsweek*, May 6, 1968)

You think of any three numbers, 747 say, and then read off the corresponding words, "synchronized digital projection." It is a device to generate verbal ornament, a machine for poetic diction. Try making up a version for whatever dialect of The Official Style you need to write — governmental, sociological, educational, psychoanalytic. Not only will it lend new resonance and authority to your prose, it will act as a multiplier, increasing length and weight. It also acts as a mechanical muse, generates inspiration, or at least serviceable instant bullshit. Produce a phrase by the three-number procedure, invent a sentence for it, and then spend a paragraph or two reflecting on what it might mean. Invent a reality to which the phrase can refer.

Let's run over the basic elements of The Official Style again. (1) It is built on *nouns,* vague, general nouns. These nouns are usually of Latin derivation, "shun" words like fixa*tion*, func*tion*, construc*tion*, educa*tion*, organiza*tion*. (2) These nouns are often, as in the game, modified by adjectives made up from other nouns like them, as in "incremental throughput" or "functional input." (3) All action is passive and impersonal. No active intransitive verbs and no direct objects. Never "I decided to fire him" but "It has been determined that the individual's continued presence in the present personnel configuration would tend to be to the detriment of the ongoing operational efficiency of the organizational unit in which the individual is currently employed." (4) Nothing is called by its ordinary name. You don't decide to bomb a town; instead, "It has been determined to maintain an aggressive and operational attack posture." You don't set up an office, you "initiate an ongoing administrative facility." (5) The status quo is preserved in syntax. All motion is converted into stasis. The Official Style denies, as much as possible, the reality of action. You don't dislike someone, you "maintain a posture of disapproval toward" him. You don't decide to hire someone, you "initiate the hiring process." Above all, you make the simple sound complex, as in the following prizewinner.

Official Style

The purpose of this project is to develop the capability for institutions of higher learning and community agencies and organizations to coalesce for the development of community services that would maximize the available resources from a number of institutions and provide communication and

Plain English

This project aims to teach universities and community organizations how to work more efficiently together.

priority needs and the
responses of the educa-
tional needs of a given
community.

Already you can see the problem. The Plain English
sounds *too* simple. A worthy project, no doubt, but who
would ever *fund* anything as obvious as that?

Official Style prose often grows from a need to say
something — to a TV camera, for example — when
nothing, or at least nothing candid, can be said. So when
a State Department spokesman is asked how the Con-
ference is going, he does not say "God knows!" but
instead:

> I think it is already possible that this particular sum-
> mit is one that is on the way to a substantial result.
> There has been evidence of an encouragingly large
> area of agreement toward a concrete and concerted
> action program by the various countries represented
> here — a program that will be concise and meaningful
> in its nature.

Maybe only the old-fashioned crooks could afford to
be candid, but such candor certainly sounds refreshing to
our bureaucratized ears. Listen to Al Capone speaking to
the press:

> I make my money by supplying a public demand. If I
> break the law, my customers, who number hundreds
> of the best people in Chicago, are as guilty as I am.
> The only difference between us is that I sell and they
> buy. Everybody calls me a racketeer. I call myself a
> business man. When I sell liquor, it's bootlegging.

When my patrons serve it on a silver tray on Lake Shore Drive, it's hospitality.

Notice how easily this passage can be read aloud? How carefully a pattern of balance is built up?

If I break the law	my customers are as guilty as I
I sell	they buy
I call myself a business man	Everybody calls me a racketeer
I sell liquor, it's bootlegging	my patrons serve it, it's hospitality

He wants you to find the pattern of his thought, not love it.

Sometimes, though, The Official Stylist is not mendacious, or even self-important, but simply absent in mind. He can write The Official Style from knee-jerk habit, like the galvanic twitch of a laboratory frog after its brain has been removed. So here, an urban planner:

The current design process was discussed and found lacking because there is no recognized programming phase; the architect is not often party to fundamental planning decisions concerning alternatives to building; the user is not a participant in design discussions. There is no behavioral design methodology, nor are there statements of accountability for decisions made, and there is no feedback mechanism or information clearinghouse. The need for a more comprehensive design process is immediate. The Behavioral Design Process is presented below in some detail as a guide to implementation of a user-oriented design methodology.

The writer is trying to say something simple but important. Into plain English, a sentence at a time, with the help of the Paramedic Method:

ORIGINAL

The current design process was discussed and found lacking because there is no recognized programming phase; (16 words)

REVISION

Current design lacks a programming phase; (6 words: LF 63%)

ORIGINAL

. . . the architect is not often party to fundamental planning decisions concerning alternatives to building; the user is not a participant in design discussions. (23 words)

REVISION

. . . neither architect nor tenant participates in fundamental planning decisions. (9 words: LF 61%)

ORIGINAL

There is no behavioral design methodology, nor are there statements of accountability for decisions made, and there is no feedback mechanism or information clearinghouse. The need for a more comprehensive design process is immediate. (34 words)

REVISION

We badly need a system which allows a designer to meet the people who will live in his design, and to learn their wishes and consider their needs. (28 words: LF 18%)

ORIGINAL

The Behavioral Design Process is presented below in some detail as a guide to implementation of a user-oriented design methodology. (21 words)

REVISION

Behavioral Design, as presented below, shows how this could be done. (11 words: LF 47%)

Now, the entire *Original:*

The current design process was discussed and found lacking because there is no recognized programming phase; the architect is not often party to fundamental planning decisions concerning alternatives to building; the user is not a participant in design discussions. There is no behavioral design methodology, nor are there statements of accountability for decisions made, and there is no feedback mechanism or information clearinghouse. The need for a more comprehensive design process is immediate. The Behavioral Design Process is presented below in some detail as a guide to implementation of a user-oriented design methodology. (94 words)

And *Revision:*

Current design lacks a programming phase; neither architect nor tenant participates in fundamental planning decisions. We badly need a system which allows a designer to meet the people who will live in his design, to learn their wishes and consider their needs. Behavioral Design, as presented below, shows how this could be done. (52 words: LF 45%)

But if buildings should be designed for people, shouldn't prose styles be too? The Official Style, often, is not. It tries to stall people, confuse them, shut them out. It deliberately hides the ball. Look at this example of The Official Style at its most anti-social. It comes from an Environmental Impact Statement which discusses the effects of jet noise on the people who live around an urban airport.

The findings of ongoing research have shown that a number of physiological effects occur under conditions of noise exposure. . . . These studies demonstrate that noise exposure does influence bodily changes, such as the so-called vegetative functions, by inhibition of gastric juices, lowered skin resistance, modified pulse rate and increased metabolism. . . .

Other studies have investigated the generalized physiological effects of noise in relation to cardiovascular disturbances, gastrointestinal problems, impairment of performance on motor tracking tasks and vascular disturbances, as well as various physical ailments. Miller (1974) states that, "Steady noise of 90 dB increases tension in all muscles." Welch (1972) concludes that "environmental sound has all-pervasive effects on the body, influencing virtually every organ system and function that has been studied," and Cohen (1971) summarized that "the distressing effects of noise alone or combined with other stress factors can eventually overwhelm man's capability for healthy adjustment with resultant physical or mental ailments. . . ."

The survey determined the presence of annoyance reactions which have been identified as indicators of stressful response to environmental noise among respondents both inside and outside the noise impact area. . . .

No need to do a detailed analysis at this stage of the game — the formula as before. In this distanced and impersonal world, no one ever suffers; they experience "the presence of annoyance reactions." And, in the report's ever-cautious style it only "appears" that the airport produces such reactions among residents.

Human beings, we need to remind ourselves here, are social beings. Our reality is a social reality. Our identity draws its felt life from our relation to other people. We become uneasy if, for extended periods of time, we neither hear nor see other people. We feel uneasy with The Official Style for the same reason. It has no human voice, no face, no personality behind it. It creates no society, encourages no social conversation. We feel that it is *unreal*. And, the "better" it is, the more true-to-type, the more unreal it becomes.

But public prose need not erase human reality. It can do just the opposite, as in the following passage from the same airport controversy — a letter from a homeowners' group president. With it, we return to human life.

Our Homeowners Association was formed about a year and a half ago principally because of an overwhelming fear of what might happen to our homes, schools and community as a result of any steps which might be taken by Lockheed and/or the City of Burbank. Our community is inexorably linked to Hollywood-Burbank Airport. The northern part of the North/South runway is in our city. . . .

Our community consists of a vast majority of single-family residences, and long-time owners with "paid in full" or "almost paid up" mortgages. We have been told, "You moved in next to the airport, it was there before you were." This is true in most cases. But, and this is a big "but"—it was an entirely different airport when most of us moved into the area. 20 to 25 years ago, the airport was "home" to small planes. We actually enjoyed watching them buzz around, and many of us spent Sunday afternoons at the airport while our children were amused watching the little planes. However, the advent of the jet plane at HBA changed the entire picture. Suddenly we were the neighbors of a Noise Factory! . . .

Our children are bombarded with noise in 2 local elementary schools, Roscoe and Glenwood. Teachers have to stop teaching until the noise passes over and everyone waits "for the next one." If the school audiometrist wants an in-depth test for a child with questionable hearing, the child must be taken away from the school altogether to eliminate outside noises.

Our backyards, streets, parks and churches, too, are inundated with noise . . . noise is an ever-constant fact of life for us. There is seldom a time when one cannot hear a plane somewhere in the vicinity—it may be "up" or it may be "down," but once a motor is turned on, we hear it!

We might well be asked, "Why do you continue to live in such a place?" Put in plain and simple terms—we have no place else to go! Years have passed and we have put more money into our mortgages and into our property. We have developed long-time friendships with neighbors and the Community. We don't want to move! . . .

Where do we go? Who is going to pay us—and how much will we be paid—for being uprooted? Who sets the price on losing a street and an entire neighborhood full of long-time friends? If 7 schools are to be closed, where do the children go? What happens to the faculty and staff at the schools? The parochial schools? The small business man who sells consumer goods — what happens when there is no one to sell to?

Plain English, in such a context, takes on almost the moral grandeur of the high style. The language of ordinary life reasserts our common humanity. Precisely the humanity, we have now come to see, The Official Style so often seeks to banish. It is a bad style, then, when it denatures human relations. When we consider that it is becoming the accepted language for the organizations that govern human relations, we can begin to see how stylistic and moral issues converge. To that convergence we must now turn.

CHAPTER FIVE

Why Bother?

I've been arguing that much of our writing problem comes from the goals and attributes that make up The Official Style. We have seen what The Official Style looks like: dominantly a noun style; a concept style; a style whose sentences have no design, no shape, rhythm, or emphasis; an unreadable, voiceless, impersonal style; a style built on euphemism and various kinds of poetic diction; above all, a style with a formulaic structure, "is" plus a string of prepositional phrases before and after. But just because it *is* a formulaic style, we can use a formula to revise it into plain English. The Paramedic Method handles the problem nicely. We might usefully review it here:

1. Circle the prepositions.
2. Circle the "is" forms.
3. Ask "Who is kicking Who?"
4. Put this "kicking" action in a simple (not compound) active verb.
5. Start fast—no mindless introductions.
6. Write out each sentence on a blank sheet of paper and mark off its basic rhythmic units with a "/".
7. Read the passage aloud with emphasis and feeling.
8. Mark off sentence lengths in the passage with a "/".

To repeat: This formula does work, but it works only because the style it aims to revise is so formulaic to begin with. It really is a *paramedic* method, an emergency procedure. Don't confuse it with the art of medicine, with knowing about the full range of English prose styles—how to recognize and how to write them. That kind of knowledge is what English composition is all about. We are talking here about a subdivision of that broader field, about only *one kind* of stylistic revision. Because it is only one kind, it leaves a lot out.

Most obviously, it leaves out time, place, and circumstance. It aims to be clear and brief, but often if the social surface is to be preserved, clarity and brevity must be measured out in small doses. We seldom communicate *only* neutral information; we are incorrigibly interested in the emotions and human relationships which go with it.

Because the Paramedic Method ignores this aspect of writing, it can get you into trouble. Well, then, you might well ask, why bother? The kind of revision we've been doing is hard work. Why do it if it's only going to get us in trouble? Why sit in your office and feel foolish trying to read a memo aloud for rhythm and shape? If The Official Style is the accepted language of our bureaucratic world, why translate it into English? Why stand up when everyone else is sitting down? Questions to be asked, though to answer we'll have to go a step or two beyond paramedicine. There are two answers, really, or rather two kinds of answers—"efficiency" answers and "ego" answers.

"Efficiency" first. A reader of the earlier version of this book made the main point for me:

> "Why Bother?" You omitted one of the most important reasons: Cost.
>
> Two years ago our new organization needed a Constitution and By-Laws, and a By-Laws Committee was appointed for the task. They found a sample from a similar organization, made title and other

changes and produced the 12-page Constitution and By-Laws. That was not sufficient, however, and they were instructed to add more "management organization" to the Constitution. But then, of course, the By-Laws didn't agree with the expanded Constitution. One By-Laws amendment corrected one disparity, but others remained. It appeared to me that when the By-Laws were expanded to match the expanded Constitution, 19 pages of that format would be required. It was getting out of hand, and the reproduction costs could break our meager treasury.

A few months ago a friend told me about *Revising Prose*, and suggested its principles might be applied to By-Laws as much as to straight prose. I was skeptical at first but I zeroed-in on Who's Kicking Who, eliminating useless words, nonsense phrases and needless repetition. And because we had never appointed all that added management organization, I simply eliminated them. The fever was catching, and I challenged myself to get it on four pages. To do that I used the left margin for headings and maximized print density by eliminating as much white area as possible. Our "lard factor" was perhaps as high as you've ever seen.

The result is our new-look Constitution and By-Laws with easily-located subjects, quicker to read with improved comprehension, and technically more accurate. One copy now costs 20¢ versus 60¢ in the original and 95¢ if we had culminated the expansions. At our most recent meeting on April 19, 1980, it was adopted unanimously with only one change: the part about Assessments was stricken completely because it had never been noticed before and, now that it was easy to see, the idea was unacceptable to the group!

A small instance for a large lesson. The cost—in money, time, perplexity—exacted by The Official Style is literally and metaphorically incalculable. If we could calculate it, though, it would certainly be the difference between 20 cents and 60 cents, and maybe between 20 cents and 95 cents. A 2/3 saving of time and money? A 4/5 saving? Whew! Imagine this kind of saving in a large corporation or government agency. These numbers may seem extravagant but the lard factor amounts to a deadly multiplier: my letter to you, two times as long as it needs to be, evokes a letter from you two times as long as mine and four times as long as the subject demands, and so on *ad infinitum*. In the context of this unforgiving multiplier, criteria like sentence shape, rhythm, and sound turn out to be less literary graces than cost-effective necessities. Reading aloud for rhythm may end up saving you money.

The reader's letter makes a second point as essential as the first—the backpressure which revision exerts on thought and imagination. Revising what we write constitutes a self-satire, a debate with ourselves. The Paramedic Method brings ideas out into the open, denies them the fulsome coloration of a special language. If the ideas are unacceptable, like the "Assessments" section of the By-Laws, we'll see this clearly. The Official Style encourages us to fool ourselves as well as other people, to believe in our own bureaucratic mysteries. The Paramedic Method puts our ideas back under real pressure. They can then develop and grow or—painful as this always is—find their way to the circular file. If translation into plain English reveals only painful banalities, it's back to the drafting board for fresh ideas. The great thing about the Paramedic Method is that it allows us to conduct this self-education *in private*.

We can, too, think of efficiency and writing in a slightly different, but not in the end less cost-effective, way. We live in an age of bureaucracy, of large and impersonal organizations, public and private. We're not likely to change this much. Size and impersonality seem unavoidable concomitants of the kind of global planning we'll increasingly have to do. But surely the task of language is to leaven rather than to echo this impersonality. It is a matter of efficiency as well as of humanity and aesthetic grace. We understand ideas better when they come, manifestly, from other human beings. That is simply the way human understanding evolved. It is people, finally, who act, not offices, or even officers.

The kind of translation into plain English we've been talking about can exert another kind of counterforce, as well. The Official Style is unrelievedly *abstract* as well as impersonal, echoes the bureaucratic preoccupation with concepts and rules. The Paramedic Method reverses the flow of this current from *concepts* back toward *objects*. It constitutes a ritual reminder to keep our feet on the ground. Dr. Johnson replied to the idealist philosopher's argument that the world exists only in our mind by kicking a stone. The Paramedic Method does much the same kind of thing for us — Who's kicking Who? The natural gravity of large organizations pulls so strongly toward concepts and abstractions that we need a formulaic counter-ritual. The Paramedic Method provides a start in this direction.

The language of bureaucracy, then, needs a cybernetic circuit to keep its dominant impetus toward impersonality and conceptual generalization in check. It ought to supply *negative* feedback, not the positive reinforcement provided by The Official Style. Such a counter-statement is not only more attractive and more fun — it's more efficient.

The "Ego" answers to "Why Bother?" come harder than the "Efficiency" arguments because they are so closely invested with questions of morality, of sincerity, hypocrisy, and the presentation of self. We might begin to sketch this answer by confronting the temptation head on. Why do all of us moralize so readily about writing style? Writing is usually described in a moral vocabulary—"sincere," "open," "devious," "hypocritical"—but is this vocabulary justified? Why do so many people feel that bad writing threatens the foundations of civilization? And why, in fact, do we think "bad" the right word to use for it? Why are we so seldom content just to call it "inefficient" and let it go at that? Why to Clarity and Brevity must we always add a discussion of "Sincerity" as well?

Let's start where "Sincerity" starts, with the primary ground for morality, the self. We may think of the self as both a dynamic and a static entity. It is static when we think of ourselves as having central, fixed selves independent of our surroundings, an "I" we can remove from society without damage, a central self inside our head. But it becomes dynamic when we think of ourselves as actors playing social roles, a series of roles which vary with the social situations in which we find ourselves. Such a social self amounts to the sum of all the public roles we play. Our complex identity comes from the constant interplay of these two selves. Our final identity is usually a mixed one, few of us being completely the same in all situations or, conversely, social chameleons who change with every context. What allows the self to grow and develop is the free interplay between these two kinds of self, the central self "inside our head" and the social self "out there." If we were completely sincere we would always say exactly what we think—and cause social chaos. If we were always acting an appropriate role, we would be either professional actors or certifiably insane. Reality, for each of us, presents itself as constant oscillation between these two extremes of interior self and social role.

When we say that writing is sincere, we mean that somehow it has managed to express this complex oscillation, this complex self. It has caught the accent of a particular self, a particular mixture of the two selves. Sincerity can't point to any *specific* verbal configuration, of course, since sincerity varies as widely as man himself. The sincere writer has not said exactly what he felt in the first words that occur to him. That might produce a revolutionary tirade or "like-you know" conversational babble. Nor has a sincere writer simply borrowed a fixed language, as when a bureaucrat writes in The Official Style. The "sincere" writer has managed to create a style which, like the social self, can become part of society, can work harmoniously in society and, at the same time, like the central self, can represent his unique selfhood. He holds his two selves in balance; this is what "authority" in writing really means.

What the act of writing involves for the writer is an integration of his self, a deliberate act of balancing its two component parts. It represents an act of socialization, and it is by repeated acts of such socialization that we become sociable beings, that we grow up. Thus, the act of writing models the presentation of self in society, constitutes a rehearsal for social reality. It is not simply a question of a preexistent self making its message known to a preexistent society. From the "Ego" point of view, it is not, initially, a question of message at all. Writing is a way to clarify, strengthen, and energize the self, to render individuality rich, full, and social. This does not mean writing that flows, as Terry Southern immortally put it, "right out of the old guts onto the goddam paper." Just the opposite. Only by taking the position of the reader toward one's own prose, putting a reader's pressure on it, can the self be made to grow. Writing can, through such pressure, enhance and expand the self, allow it to try out new possibilities, tentative selves. We return here to the backpressure revision exerts. It stimulates not only the mind but the whole personality. We are not simply offering an idea but our personality as context for that idea. And just as revision makes our ideas grow and develop, it encourages us to see the different ways we can act in society, the alternative paths to socialize the self.

The moral ingredient in writing, then, works first not on the morality of the message but on the nature of the sender, on the complexity of the self. "Why bother?" To invigorate and enrich your selfhood, to increase, in the most literal sense, your self-consciousness. Writing, properly pursued, does not make you better. It makes you more alive, more coherent, more in control. A mind thinking, not a mind asleep. It aims, that is, not to denature the human relationship that writing sets up, but to enhance and enrich it. It is not trying to squeeze out the expression of personality but to make such expression possible, not trying to obscure all record of a particular occasion and its human relationships, but to make them maximally clear. Again, this is why we worry so much about bad writing. It signifies incoherent people, failed social relationships. This worry makes sense only if we feel that writing, ideally, should express human relationships and feelings, not abolish them.

From the "Ego" point of view, then, we revise The Official Style when it fails to socialize the self and hence to enrich it, to discipline the Ego to the surrounding egos which give it meaning. This, unhappily, is most of the time. Pure candor can be soundly destructive but so can pure formula, endless cliché. When formula takes over, self and society depart. The joy goes out of the prose. It's no fun to write. And when this happens, you get those social gaffes, those trodden toes, those "failures of communication" which so often interfere with the world's business. The human feeling which has been pushed out the front door sneaks in the back. So when you cease to feel good about what you write, when you cease to add something of yourself to it, watch out!

When we try to put these two answers to "Why Bother?" together, we discover a paradoxical convergence. Cases do exist where one answer will do by itself — in the By-Laws case, for example, the "Efficiency" argument really is all we need — but more often than not the two kinds of justification support one another. The "Efficiency" argument, pressed hard enough, comes to overlap the "Ego" argument and vice versa. We may, in this area of overlap, have come across the richness we feel when we use all the customary value-laden terms to describe a piece of prose — "sincere," "honest," "fresh," "straightforward," etc. We feel that somehow Ego and Efficiency have come to collaborate in establishing a clarity that makes understanding a pleasure and a shared one.

At this point, the paramedic analogy breaks down. Beyond paramedicine lies medicine; beyond the specific analysis of a specific style — what we have been doing here — lies the study of style in general. Verbal style can no more be fully explained by a set of rules, stylistic or moral, than can any other kind of human behavior. Intuition, *trained* intuition, figures as strongly in the one as in the other. You must learn how to see.

You'll then be able to answer the fundamental question which this chapter — and this book — can only introduce. *How* to revise The Official Style is easy — a piece of cake. As we've seen, anyone can do it. The questions which generate no rules, the questions which try our judgment — and our goodness — are *When?* and *Why?*.

APPENDIX: TERMS

You can see things you don't know the names for but in prose style as in everything else it is easier to see what you know how to describe. The psychological ease that comes from calling things by their proper names has been much neglected in such writing instruction as still takes place. As a result, inexperienced writers often find themselves reduced to talking about "smoothness," "flow," and other meaningless generalities when they are confronted by a text. And so here are some basic terms.

PARTS OF SPEECH

In traditional English grammar, there are eight parts of speech: verbs, nouns, pronouns, adjectives, adverbs, prepositions, conjunctions, interjections. *Grammar*, in its most general sense, refers to all the rules which govern how meaningful statements can be made in any language. *Syntax* refers to sentence structure, to word order. *Diction* means simply word choice. *Usage* means linguistic custom.

Verbs

1. Verbs have two voices, active and passive:
   An *active verb* indicates the subject acting:
      Jack *kicks* Bill.
   A *passive verb* indicates the subject acted upon:
      Bill *is kicked* by Jim.

91

2. Verbs come in three moods: indicative, subjunctive, and imperative: A verb in the *indicative mood* says that something is a fact. If it asks a question, it is a question about a fact:
   Jim *kicks* Bill. *Has* Jim *kicked* Bill yet?

   A verb in the *subjunctive mood* says that something is a wish or thought rather than a fact:
   If Jim *were* clever, he *would* trick Bill.

   A verb in the *imperative mood* issues a command:
   Jim, *kick* Bill!

3. A verb can be either *transitive* or *intransitive*.
   A *transitive verb* takes a direct object:
   Jim kicks *Bill*.

   An *intransitive verb* does not take a direct object. It represents action without a specific goal:
   Jim *runs* with great gusto.

   The verb "to be" ("is," "was," etc.) is often a *linking verb* because it links subject and predicate without transmitting a specific action:
   Jim *is* a skunk.

4. English verbs have six tenses: present, past, present perfect, past perfect, future, and future perfect:

   > Present: Jim *kicks* Bill. (Present progressive: Jim *is kicking* Bill.)
   > Past: Jim *kicked* Bill.
   > Present perfect: Jim *has kicked* Bill.
   > Past perfect: Jim *had kicked* Bill.
   > Future: Jim *will kick* Bill.
   > Future perfect: Jim *will have kicked* Bill.

The present perfect, past perfect, and future perfect are called *compound tenses.*

5. Verbs in English have three so-called *infinitive forms: infinitive, participle,* and *gerund.* These verb forms often function as adjectives or nouns.

Infinitive: To kick Jim makes great sport. ("To kick" is here the subject of "makes.")

Participles and gerunds have the same form; where the form is used as an adjective, it is called a *participle,* when used as a noun, a *gerund.*

Participles. Present participle: Jim is in a truly *kicking* mood. Past participle: Bill was a very well-*kicked fellow.*

Gerund: Kicking Bill is an activity hugely enjoyed by Jim.

(When a word separates the "to" in an infinitive form its complementary form, as in "to directly stimulate" instead of "to stimulate," the infinitive is said to be a *split infinitive.* Most people think this ought not to be done unless absolutely necessary.)

Verbs which take "it" or "there" as subjects are said to be in an *impersonal construction,* e.g., "It has been decided to fire him" or "There has been a personnel readjustment."

Nouns

A noun names something or somebody. A proper noun names a particular being—Jim.
1. Number. The singular number refers to one ("a cat"), plural to more than one ("five cats").
2. Collective nouns. Groups may be thought of as a single unit, as in "the army."

Pronouns

A pronoun is a word used instead of a noun. There are different kinds:

1. Personal pronouns—e.g., I, me, you, he, him, them
2. Intensive pronouns—e.g., myself, yourself, himself
3. Relative pronouns—e.g., who, which, that. These must have *antecedents,* words they refer back to. "Jim has a talent (antecedent) which (relative pronoun) Bill does not possess."
4. Indefinite pronouns—e.g., somebody, anybody, anything
5. Interrogative pronouns—e.g., who?, what?

Possessives

Singular: A worker's hat. Plural: The workers' hats. ("It's," however, equals "it is." The possessive is "its.")

Adjectives

An *adjective* modifies a noun, e.g., "Jim was a *good* hiker."

Adverbs

An *adverb* modifies a verb, e.g., "Jim kicked *swiftly.*"

Prepositions

A *preposition* connects a noun or pronoun with a verb, an adjective, or another pronoun, e.g., "I ran *into* her arms" or "The girl *with* the blue scarf."

Conjunctions

Conjunctions join sentences or parts of them. There are two kinds, coordinating and subordinating.

1. Coordinating conjunctions—e.g., and, but, or, for—connect statements of equal status, e.g., "Bill ran and Jim fell" or "I got up but soon fell down."

2. Subordinating conjunctions—e.g., that, who, when—connect a main clause with a subordinate one, e.g., "I thought *that* he had gone."

Interjection

A sudden outcry, e.g., "Wow!"

SENTENCES

Every sentence must have both a subject and verb, stated or implied, e.g., "Jim (subject) kicks (verb)."

Three kinds

1. A *declarative sentence* states a fact, e.g., "Jim kicks Bill."
2. An *interrogative sentence* asks a question, e.g., "Did Jim kick Bill?"
3. An *exclamatory sentence* registers an exclamation, e.g., "Like, I mean, you know, like wow!"

Three basic structures

1. A *simple sentence* makes one self-standing assertion, i.e., has one main clause, e.g., "Jim kicks Bill."
2. A *compound sentence* makes two or more self-standing assertions, i.e., has two main clauses, e.g., "Jim kicks Bill and Bill feels it" or "Jim kicks Bill and Bill feels it and Bill kicks back."
3. A *complex sentence* makes one self-standing assertion and one or more dependent assertions, subordinate clauses, dependent on the main clause, e.g., "Jim, who has been kicking Bill these twenty-five years, kicks him still and, what's more, still enjoys it."

In *compound sentences*, the clauses are connected by *coordinating conjunctions,* in *complex sentences* by *subordinating conjunctions.*

Restrictive and nonrestrictive relative clauses

A restrictive clause modifies directly, and so restricts the meaning of the antecedent it refers back to, e.g., "This is the tire *which blew out on the freeway.*" One specific tire is intended. In such clauses the relative clause is *not* set off by a comma.

A nonrestrictive clause, though still a dependent clause, does not directly modify its antecedent and is set off by commas. "These tires, which are quite expensive, last a very long time."

Appositives

An *appositive* is an amplifying word or phrase placed next to the term it refers to and set off by commas, e.g., "Henry VIII, *a glutton for punishment*, had six wives."

NOUN STYLE AND VERB STYLE

Every sentence must have a noun and a verb, but one can be emphasized, sometimes almost to the exclusion of the other. The Official Style — strings of prepositional phrases and "is" — exemplifies a noun style *par excellence*. Here are three examples, the first of a noun style, the second of a verb style, and the third of a balanced noun-verb mixture.

Noun Style

There is in turn a two-fold structure of this "binding-in." In the first place, by virtue of internalization of the standard, conformity with it tends to be of personal, expressive and/or instrumental significance to ego. In the second place, the structuring of the reactions of alter to ego's action as sanctions is a function of his conformity with the standard. Therefore conformity as a direct mode of the fulfillment of his own need-dispositions tends to coincide with the conformity as a condition of eliciting the favorable and avoiding the unfavorable reactions of others. (Talcott Parsons, *The Social System* [Glencoe, Ill.: Free Press, 1951], p. 38)

Verb Style

Patrols, sweeps, missions, search and destroy. It contined every day as if part of sunlight itself. I went to the colonel's briefings every day. He explained how effectively we were keeping the enemy off balance, not allowing them to move in, set up mortar sites, and gather for attack. He didn't seem to hate them. They were to him like pests or insects that had to be kept away. It seemed that one important purpose of patrols was just for them to take place, to happen, to exist; there had to be patrols. It gave the men something to do. Find the enemy, make contact, kill, be killed, and return. Trap, block, hold. In the first five days, I lost six corpsmen — two killed, four wounded. (John A. Parrish, *12, 20 & 5: A Doctor's Year in Vietnam* [Baltimore: Penguin Books, 1973], p. 235)

Mixed Noun-Verb Style

We know both too much and too little about Louis XIV ever to succeed in capturing the whole man. In externals, in the mere business of eating, drinking, and dressing, in the outward routine of what he loved to call the *metier du roi*, no historical character, not even Johnson or Pepys, is better known to us; we can even, with the aid of his own writings, penetrate a little of the majestic facade which is *Le Grand Roi*. But when we have done so, we see as in a glass darkly. Hence the extraordinary number and variety of judgments which have been passed upon him; to one school, he is incomparably the ablest ruler in modern European history; to another, a mediocre blunderer, pompous, led by the nose by a succession of generals and civil servants; whilst to a third, he is no great king, but still the finest actor of royalty the world has ever seen. (W. H. Lewis, *The Splendid Century: Life in the France of Louis XIV* [N.Y.: Anchor Books, 1953], p. 1)

For further explanation of the basic terms of grammar, see George O. Curme's *English Grammar* in the Barnes & Noble College Outline Series.